TOM SHIELDS

FREE AT LAST

TOM SHIELDS

MAINSTREAM PUBLISHING

EDINBURGH AND LONDON

ACKNOWLEDGEMENT

The author would like to thank the staff at the Inland Revenue and Rutherford & Macpherson, sheriff officers, without whose letters of encouragement this book might never have been written.

Copyright © Tom Shields, 1997

First published in 1997 by
MAINSTREAM PUBLISHING COMPANY (EDINBURGH) LTD
7 Albany Street
Edinburgh EH1 3UG

ISBN 1 85158 880 9

A catalogue record for this book is available from the British Library

Typeset in Plantin
Printed and bound in Great Britain by Butler and Tanner Ltd

CONTENTS

DEDICATION

David Shaw was larger than life. He was an advertising man and a showman. He had on his office wall in Park Circus, Glasgow, an award from an advertising trade magazine declaring him to be the Most Passionate Scotsman of the Year 1990. But his real passion was theatre in his capacity as director of the Pantheon amateur drama company.

Driven by David, Pantheon used to fill the King's Theatre in Glasgow with huge audiences that professional companies could only dream of. David never produced or directed a bad show. At least as far as he was concerned. He quoted me as saying of one of his shows: 'The best night out ever experienced in Glasgow.' I seem to recall saying: 'This is not exactly the best night out ever experienced in Glasgow.' But never mind.

When I challenged him that his Brownshirt thugs in *Cabaret* were less than convincing he replied: 'It's not easy getting people from Newton Mearns to play Nazis.'

The man Shaw himself was no mean performer. He officiated as Bud Neill cartoon character Big Chief Toffy Teeth at the unveiling of the Lobey Dosser statue. At a Burns Supper in the Doublet Bar – pubs were his other performance space – David treated us to a dissertation on houghmagandie. His first sexual tryst took place in a field. His abiding memory was that the encounter took place on top of a mound of grass cuttings. He added that ever since he has not been able to look at a newly mown lawn without experiencing a certain frisson. 'I've got the best-kept grass in Giffnock,' he claimed. 'I'm the only guy I know who takes in lawns.'

I suspect that David Shaw has already formed a Pantheon up there and is casting for his first musical. 'Jesus,' he'll be saying, 'I can make you a superstar.'

David Shaw died on 17 November, 1996

OVERHEARD

PROOF, if proof were needed, that headmasters regard themselves as god-like figures. A heidie, name withheld to protect the egotistical, was haranguing the weans at assembly when he uttered the words: 'As Jesus Christ said and, I think, rightly . . .'

ELECTION soundbite. Paul Cullen, Solicitor-General and Tory candidate in Eastwood, overheard explaining to a party worker the difference between being a lawyer and a politician: 'As an advocate you're trained to answer questions directly and precisely but as a politician that's the last thing you do.' Mr Cullen lost.

DURING a Glasgow rally against the Criminal Justice Bill, a dangerous radical says to fellow dangerous radical: 'Oh no, there's the TV cameras. If my mother sees me smoking she'll kill me.'

IN the Malmaison restaurant,

Glasgow: A young man asking the waiter what exactly were these *pommes purees* on the menu. On being told, the young man expressed some relief. He had thought

7

they were 'thae wee smelly dried flooers'.

IN a bar in Troon, two strangers having a chat. After the usual pleasantries, one says to the other: 'And what is it you do for a living?' 'I work in air traffic control,' is the reply. 'Well, you've made a right arse of Ayr town centre,' is the response.

A HOTEL guest discussing how luxurious had been his accommodation: 'The bathrobe was that fluffy I could hardly get it into my case. I had to leave the towels.'

IN Airdrie a lady discusses her new medication with a friend: 'See these new tablets? I feel great. They've taken 10 years off my life.'

IN a Scrabster hotel where two Glasgow offshore oil workers are bemoaning the change of the management of their rig to an Italian company: 'Whit's the Latin for spanner, anyway?'

DEPARTMENT of Tenuous Claims To Fame: Overheard in the National Galleries, three Edinburgh ladies admiring the fine paintings of Sir William McTaggart. The first lady turns to the second and says: 'Did you know that my mother's teeth were made by his sister?'

IN a Kilwinning supermarket. Wife to husband: 'No, don't bother getting any grapes. The weans just eat them.'

ARCHETYPAL Scottish homophobe: 'At one time it was a criminal offence to be a practising homosexual in this country. Then it was made legal for consenting adults over 21. Now the age is down to 18 and some people want to make it 16. I think I'll emigrate before they make it compulsory.'

ON Radio Clyde in the wee small hours, a conversation between DJ Bobby Haines and a young female caller. Asked what was the last film she had seen, the caller said *Cliffhanger*. To which DJ Haines asked, 'Is that Stallone?' 'Naw,' she replied, 'It finished last Sa'urday.'

IN a hostelry in Rothesay: 'Jimmy's away up the road to meet his new girlfriend.' 'What's she like?' 'Ah'll no says she's getting on but she cut the breid at the Last Supper.'

THE stricture about not getting your pudding until you have finished your greens appears to have been supplanted by this overheard instruction from a young mother to her offspring as they perambulated along a shopping mall: 'Don't eat your sweets till you've had your chips.'

CAN anyone out there confirm

the folk legend of the radio presenter who set the quiz question 'Who sang "Boom Bang-a-Bang" in the Eurovision song contest?' and asked listeners to mark their entries 'Lulu contest'?

A LADY whose aged aunt died during a bank holiday weekend and who had to wait until Tuesday to register the details: 'You would have thought that they could have had a skeleton staff in to deal with the deaths over the weekend.'

AN American tourist to his wife as their train passes Murrayfield Stadium, hallowed home of Scottish rugby: 'That's where they hold the soccer riots.'

IN the bar of the Tufted Duck Hotel in St Coombs, Fraserburgh, the following conversation between a deeply Doric barmaid and two visitors from somewhere south of Watford: 'Fit are you boys hae'in then?' 'Do you have any real ale?' 'Ahinny.' 'Good. We'll have two small whiskies and two halves of the Ahinny.'

ON a British Airways flight from Mexico City to Heathrow, a German passenger asking if he could possibly move to a better seat next to the one he'd been allocated. The stewardess replied that they were still waiting for some passengers to board but added: 'Why don't you put your towel on it?'

AN argument regarding the relative merits of Montrose and Gourdon featured this retort: 'At

least in Gourdon we dinna ca feesh fush?'

ON the What Would You Do If You Won the Lottery Front: 'I'd go straight to Ross Hall private hospital.' 'Why, what's wrong with you?' 'Nothing. I'd book my liver transplant in advance.'

A CRUEL but accurate description of a person who is not exactly the life and soul of the party: 'He deprives you of solitude without providing you with company.'

RACIST comments are still sadly all too common of an evening in Scotland's ethnic restaurants. We hear of an example from a Chinese eating establishment in one of the nether regions of Edinburgh, where a callow youth has entered the premises just after pub closing and is in search of some sustenance. He places his order by pulling at the side of both eyes to achieve a slant-eyed effect and uttering: 'Sweet and sour chicken with fried rice.'

The Chinese waiter places his fingers above and below his eyes and, pulling to achieve a round-eyed effect, sent him off with a well-known two-word phrase ending in 'off'.

AMID the sales scramble in Fraser's, Glasgow. Elderly lady to assistant: 'Excuse me, are these umbrellas waterproof?'

SO what are the similarities between a priest and a pint of

Guinness, we were asked. We didn't know.

First of all, the appearance – black with a white collar. And if you get a bad one you can have a really sore arse the next morning.

THE row over Glasgow cooncillors soliciting free trips has had serious consequences for the reputation of James Mutter, the City Chambers tribune for the people of the Hutchesontown ward.

'See a' that stuff about junkets,' opined a Gorbals lady. 'Ah never knew Cooncillor Mutter was oan drugs.'

A MEMBER of Arlington Baths Club in Glasgow bemoaning the passing of old traditions: 'Men would drop their pants where they stood and left them because they knew Robert the pant boy would pick them up and take them to the laundry . . . It's a sign of the times that we don't have a pant boy anymore.'

TWO women in a Highland village. The subject is their new minister.

1ST LADY: 'Have you heard the new minister?'
2ND LADY: 'No.'
1ST LADY: 'Bawls like a bull.'
2ND LADY: 'Has he?'

A CIVIC dignitary at the official opening of a new Royal Society for the Prevention of Cruelty to Animals veterinary clinic at Birkenhead on Merseyside. It was a great improvement on the previous premises, the dignitary said: 'In the last place there was no room to swing a cat.'

A NEWLY married couple, in receipt of a gift of a not expensive but perfectly acceptable tea service, expressed their gratitude by saying: 'It's just what we need. We've been having to use a good set.'

JOURNALISTS who turned up at the Strathclyde police news

11

conference for the chief constable's annual report were confronted by an impressive display of drugs hard, soft, and recreational. The table, laden with samples of such substances as Temazepam, Temgesic, heroin, cannabis in its various forms, cocaine, amphetamines, and ecstasy, was intended as an illustration of the drugs which blight our society.

Reevel Alderson, the notoriously humorous correspondent of BBC Scotland, was deeply impressed. 'I was just expecting coffee and biscuits,' he said.

MICHAEL Parkinson recalled a signing session in a Wolverhampton bookshop where a 'fan club' of elderly ladies turned up, gazed taciturnly at him throughout the event, and left without buying a book.

'I'll tell you what,' said one of the exiting fan club. 'He doesn't suit the daylight.'

WEE STORIES

A THESIS by a medical student explored the similarity between wounds suffered by patients at Glasgow hospital casualty units and those suffered by combatants in medieval battles. The thesis was titled *Just an Ordinary Sword*. The title was inspired by an interview with a patient who was admitted with a number of lacerations to his back. Asked what weapon his assailant used, he replied that it was a sword. Asked further what kind of sword, he replied: 'Just an ordinary sword.' You know, the kind all the men in Glasgow carry as a matter of course.

Another case history quoted was a lady who came in with a hatchet embedded in her skull. She appeared perfectly calm and was, in fact, making small talk with the nurses. Including the comment: 'You must see some right sights in here.'

THERE was an old lady who wanted to buy a certain parrot but

the pet shop owner would not sell it to her.

'Madam,' he said, 'It is a foul-mouthed parrot. His vile language would only upset visitors to your home.'

The lady persisted. She had a plan to cure the parrot of his constant use of bad language. 'Every time you swear,' she says to the parrot, 'I will put you in the freezer for 30 seconds.'

The parrot is duly purchased and the lady is taking her new charge home by taxi. The taxi is caught up in a traffic jam.

'What's the f****** hold-up?'

asks the parrot. When they get home the parrot is punished by being popped into the freezer.

He emerges 30 seconds later, shivering, and says: 'That was bloody freezing. But, tell me missus, what the f*** did the turkey do?'

THERE are some stories which are better told exactly as they come to the Diary.

John I. Thomson of Glasgow wrote: 'I earn a living as a freelance radio producer. Recently I was in Govan to do some tape recording. I was walking along a street between Govan Road and Golspie Avenue when I noticed a strange creature, dead, lying on the ground. It reminded me of the creature from Alien. I was about to move on when I was joined by a man and a woman.

"Do you know what that is?" asked the woman. I shook my head. "It's a lizard. Something's went and ate a lizard. Still," she continued, "that's Govan for you," and walked on.'

FROM deepest Ayrshire, from Dreghorn in fact, we heard of a geography exam in which pupils were asked to define some very basic terms. One youngster was doing well. The galaxy, he said, was 'the sun, the moon, the planets, the stars – everything'. An ocean was 'a vast area of sea between continents'. Then we

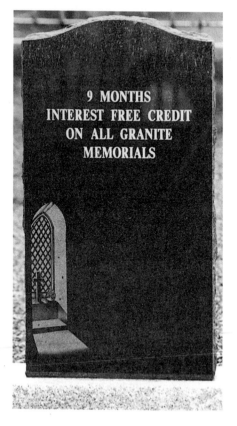

9 MONTHS INTEREST FREE CREDIT ON ALL GRANITE MEMORIALS

have: 'Continent – able to control one's urination and defecation; sexually chaste.'

BRITISH Rail were doing some electrification work on the line between Saltcoats and Glasgow. The normal service was broken at Kilwinning and passengers were transferred to a waiting coach which took them to Johnstone. There, they reboarded the train for the remainder of the journey. The coach was duly flagged down by a wee Kilwinning wumman. As the coach door glides open she asks the driver, 'Hey, son! Is this a bus or a train?' The driver replies, 'It's a train.' 'Thank God,' says the wee wumman. 'I thought I'd missed it.'

A FEATURE of the new improved National Health Service is the penchant for hospital trusts to put advertisements in any and every document to hand. We can understand why the Royal Alexandra Hospital in Paisley urges patients to get their will done by McMahon the local solicitors. The ad for Valhalla Pets Cremations Ltd – 'for the dignity and respect your pet deserves' – is less easy to get a handle on.

A COPY of a letter from Scottish Provident, the life insurance and pension people, to a school in Fife passes across our desk. It is a reply to an invitation to participate in a management training conference for the pupils. The letter says: 'As we do not run a management training programme we would therefore have difficulty in targeting a meaningful presentation.' The letter is signed 'Nia Parry, Management Trainer'.

Confused? So were the school.

A BOOK published by the national Council of Churches in the Philippines has been brought to our attention. It is called *Axiology and Teleology of the Epistemology, Missiology and Praxiology of Human Rights: Understanding Nature, Society, Culture and Consciousness*. It has chapters on such subjects as Thinking and Being: the Chicken and the Egg, Empirio-Criticism or Machism, and the Implications of Gnosiology. We were going to serialise this tome in the Diary but settled, instead, for the concluding paragraph: 'Clearly, there is a close relationship between being and thinking. One has to think well in order to express well natural, kingdomistic, interspeciesistic, human, social, and class realities. Hence, one must have a careful axiology and teleology of

the epistemology, missiology, and praxiology of human rights. Then and only then can one engage in a meaningful discourse or debate with others on questions related to human rights matters.'

We couldn't agree more.

EXTRACT from the rules for the Hennessy awards for up-and-coming Irish writers: 'To be eligible for consideration, stories and poems must first be chosen for publication in "New Irish Writing", which appears on the first Sunday of every Monday in the *Sunday Tribune*.'

DEPT of We Know What She Meant: The Government announced that it is finally to ban the export of land mines, which have caused millions of deaths all over the world. Ann Clwyd, Labour MP and campaigner for such a ban, said: 'It's a step in the right direction.'

ONE of the bedrooms in the Glen Mhor Hotel in Inverness is called the Prince Charles suite. It is so-called because the Prince of Wales once had breakfast there. The room was subsequently turned into a romantic boudoir complete with four-poster bed. It is perhaps a simile for the state of royal romance these days that beneath the canopy in the Prince Charles suite there is no longer a four-poster fit for a royal couple but two single beds.

DONALD Dewar received a call from the BBC television drama department at Pebble Mill in Birmingham. No, they didn't want the MP for Glasgow Garscadden to play Heathcliffe in a remake of *Wuthering Heights*, although we believe he could make a pretty good stab at it. They were making a play in which a police inspector enters a room and says the line: 'Switch off that TV. What's that boring nonsense you were watching anyway?'

The boring bit on TV the Pebble Mill producers wanted to use was Donald talking about devolution on the Kilroy show. Was that all right? they asked. Donald, ever the gentleman, agreed.

DEMOCRACY in action, this time from the Western Isles Council debating chamber in Stornoway. Councillor Donald Maclean, the member for Lochmaddy, declared that he did not understand a report to the finance committee. Despite attempted explanations by the chief executive and the director of finance, Councillor Maclean, a retired police super-intendent, declared himself 'still confused'. Some longer-serving council members told Mr Maclean not to worry and that he would soon pick things up. Mr Maclean stood his ground: 'I accept what the director of finance has said but I am still confused. However, I reserve the right to be confused. That is my right and it is my intention every time I am confused to not keep quiet. And no one on this council will make me keep quiet – whatever their title – when I am confused.'

And it wasn't even in the Gaelic.

A CROCK OF WEE STORIES

THE BBC Scotland comedy series *The High Life* with Siobhan Redmond, Forbes Masson and Alan Cunningham was described thus in the BBC *Worldwide* magazine: 'Poised at the end of the runway, this comedy concerns the antics of an Air Scotia shuttle crew based at the fictional Prestwick Airport . . .' The BBC mag obviously knew something about dear old half-empty Prestwick that the airport operators themselves have yet to admit.

LESLEY Riddoch, editor of the Scotswoman newspaper, was on the BBC Breakfast programme being strident, as she does so well, about International Women's Day. She chose the wrong person with whom to be strident, Sir Bernard Ingham, the doughty former media adviser to Mrs Thatcher, who was on the programme to review the daily papers. 'Do you have any children and if so, who's looking after them right now?' she asked.

'Yes. One. Himself. He's 38,' replied Sir Bernard.

THE scene was Queen Street Station in Glasgow where shivering passengers were waiting for an Edinburgh train which had been much delayed due to that wrong kind of snow, which seems to paralyse the railways. Those nice people from ScotRail announced that passengers, when they finally got on the train, were to be given a free cheering cup of tea or coffee. A young lady passenger asked the trolley chap for her free cuppa and was duly furnished with one. 'But,' he announces, 'the man opposite cannot have a cup.' Why not? 'Well, I don't have enough hot water for everybody and the conductor told me to look after the women and children first,' he said.

THERE'S nothing like a hip replacement to get the conversation going, as our old friend Bill Waddell from Cumbernauld found out. He was recovering from such an operation, when he bumped (but not literally, we hope) into a wee wumman who set about reassuring him at great length about the efficacy of a 'hip transplant'. Like everyone else, she knew someone who had had one and was now enjoying a new lease of life. And she added: 'It amazes me that these donors can go on living a normal life wi' just the one hip.'

DEPT of A Nation Once Again: Heinz have a range of traditional farmhouse soups which, naturally, includes scotch broth. Purchasers of tins of the aforementioned broth learn from the label that it is 'inspired by traditional English country cooking'.

LET us introduce a Glasgow writer name of Hughie Healy who has published his own book. He came to the writing late in life, apparently, after life as a merchant seaman. But Hughie's introduction spoke for itself: 'In 1989 I threw aside a half-read novel by a well-known Scottish writer. With the humility for which I am renowned, I declared to anyone who would listen, "I can write better f***** stories than that."' (We should point out that the lack of the final asterisk back there has to do with Hughie's particular and perverse approach to spelling.)

He added: 'My literary experiences at that time consisted of writing letters of apology and pleas of guilty.' Well-qualified then was our man to join the new robust school of Glasgow writers.

The book is called *Who Needs Orgasms!* The content is raw, random, and ranting but is the work of a true original. Puritans need not fear the title. It is not a reference to sex but to the sheer joy Hughie experienced when he landed a haymaker punch and laid-low an East End ned.

We liked this short piece: 'She brought her culture and mystique to my city street. This Asian mother and child. The exotic colours of her shalwer-kalmeez, highlighted brown skin and dark eyes. Her lips moved in prayer perhaps to a different god than mine. The little one spoke words I

failed to comprehend. She answered in the universal language of mothers: "I'm oot withoot any money so shut your face. You're getting nae crisps." '

A STRAW poll of staff on the subject of what tune to choose for the telephone-hold jingle at the Falkirk offices of the Child Support Agency ended in a close tie between 'Stand by your Man' and 'Money, Money, Money'.

THE proselytising by Helen Liddell, the Monklands East MP, against the excess consumption of Buckfast has not gone unnoticed by her constituents. Mrs Liddell has even replaced a certain chap called Jimmy in the annals of

rhyming slang. Monklands youths who need to take a leak while indulging in a spot of alfresco Buckie-drinking can be heard to say that they are popping behind the bushes for 'a quick Helen'.

DEPT of We Know What They Meant. A nice lady on Clyde 2 radio finished her road report with this warning about flooding: 'If you are passing water today, please do so with extreme caution.'

HUGH Wilson of the West End of Glasgow tells of a raffle in which he was asked to participate. It was a good cause, the object being to raise funds for an old folks home in Clydebank. The cash was to be used to buy special chairs for residents suffering from incontinence. First prize was two tickets for a concert by Wet, Wet, Wet.

A KILMARNOCK lady who has the Gaelic writes to tell us how amused she was to find some Gaeltachd graffiti (apparently approved and inserted by the management) in the ladies toilet at the Princes Square shopping centre in Glasgow. It reads: *Phaigh mi sgillin's cha do rinn mi ach breum.* Which, as we are sure you know, roughly translates as: 'Here I sit broken-hearted, paid a shilling and only farted.'

RAYMOND Robertson, when he was Tory MP for Aberdeen South, had the important but onerous task of seconding the Queen's speech. The occasion is an opportunity for an up-and-coming back bencher to make his or her mark. The tone has to be light-hearted, witty, but with undertones of gravitas. And the boy Raymond done good, if a congratulatory fax from a colleague was anything to go by. It was 'a stylish, amusing, and well-marshalled speech', wrote Jonathan Aitken, who at the time was Tory MP for Thanet South and the Paris Ritz. 'I feel optimistic about your promotion prospects after such a bravura performance.' Kind words, indeed. But spoiled somewhat by the fact that the fax was sent to one

George Robertson, the Labour chap. And the message was dated the day before Raymond actually made the speech.

THE upmarket café of the CCA arts centre in Glasgow is the sort of place where wild mushrooms often come *en feuille* on a bed of cracked wheat. A young lady was asked what she would like to drink. She could not decide between white wine or fizzy water. She eventually asks for 'half and half'. Some time later the waitress returned with a half-pint of heavy and a whisky.

SPOTTED, in fact extremely hard to miss, at the A82 turn-off for Clydebank Crematorium, a huge billboard advertising Sky TV with this comforting message for grieving relatives: 'Live coverage of the Ashes.'

THE scene was a school in darkest Lanarkshire, where teacher had asked her little charges to write a short story about the weather. To help them, she has written a list of useful words, including windy. Thus one of the offerings: 'The windy cleaner cums tae ma bit but it's too windy tae wash the windys.'

We were not sure whether the following event came into the category of Haud Me Back or Book Me a Seat in the Front Row.

**VOTE
HECKLER - Town Clerk
RICH - Treasurer**

The what's on guide to Renfrew District Council museums and art galleries revealed that the members of the Paisley Philosophical Institution were to be treated to a lecture entitled 'Amateur Gynaecology for Beginners'. The talk was being delivered by a Dr James Black, who hails from Kilmarnock, which goes some way to explaining the unusual nature of the event. A spokeslady from the Paisley Philosophical Institution told us that the lecture was not what it seems. It was 'tongue in cheek'. We preferred not to subject the matter to closer examination. Except to comment that it would have been nice to avail oneself of a working knowledge of the subject. If only to be able to say: 'Let me through, I'm a gynaecologist' when we came across a medical emergency.

FROM Dundee we heard a tale which proved that sexual discrimination is still rampant in Clootie City.

The scene is a hostelry in the Hilltown district. Mine host is aghast to discover that there have been some goings-on of an intimate nature in the WC compartment of his establishment. A chap and a chapess, overcome with lust, had locked themselves into said compartment and had, well, been at it. So much so that the toilet seat was broken during the tryst. Mine host was so affronted that he took the Draconian action of banning the lady who had been involved.

Why ban the lady and not the gentleman, was a question on many Dundonian lips? Could it be that the chap in question was a big spender, an economic asset? No, explained mine host. Logically, the woman was at fault because she had affronted the Dundonian code of decency by disporting herself in the gents. If the chap had been caught in the ladies, he would have faced expulsion.

A NAE Luck award to Mackie Academy, Stonehaven, secondary school, whose pupils witnessed an

unrehearsed lesson in practical biology during a fund-raising event. The idea was to let loose two docile-looking beasts in a field marked out in squares, and punters were invited to bet on the position of the first deposit of a cowpat. Sadly the academy's answer to the national lottery had to be abandoned when the frisky pair spotted a bull in the next field and took off in udder-juddering pursuit.

WE were puzzled by a piece of graffiti spotted recently in Glasgow which urged: 'F*** the Pope and Pakis with Sherpa vans.' What is the agenda here? Are white people who drive Sherpa vans acceptable? Does the Pope drive a Sherpa van?

A DOSE OF WEE STORIES

TRULY wondrous are these wee pocket computers. Addresses, phone numbers, all sorts of information available at the touch of a button. An advocate of the Diary's acquaintance has a file on his pocket computer listing those people who are in his debt. Simply keying in the three letters PAV brings up on screen a list of friends who have touched him recently for some folding stuff and have not yet repaid. PAV is short for Pavarotti and a Pavarotti is, of course, an outstanding tenner.

LORNE VAN SINCLAIR
Outstanding in his field
**Specializing in Rural &
Vacation Property**

WE have, we believe, an entirely accurate transcript of a telephone call made to the Inverness area between a shootin' landowner and his gamekeeper. It was at a time when the shootin' was rather thin due to a lack of targets.
LANDOWNER: 'And how are the grouse?'
GAMEKEEPER: 'They're both very well so far, sir.'

WE had never thought of Elie in Fife as being an especially up-market place. But it must be. In its newsletter, the Elie Sports Club informed members that family membership does not include *au pairs*.

FUNERALS should be a time for quiet dignity but in these modern times it is not always so. We heard

of a young chap who came up with the bright suggestion of making a video of the funeral service and cremation of an aged relative 'so that we can send it to the people who can't be there'.

In another case, two relatives went along to the church to make arrangements for the funeral service of a dearly departed mother. After the hymns had been agreed the son-in-law, a keen piper, asked if it would be appropriate for him to play some pipe music as the corpse was being taken out of church. Before the minister could express an opinion, an exasperated niece interjected: 'What do you think it is? A bloody haggis?'

A NEW bus fare system in Aberdeen required passengers to state their destination when they boarded. 'A 14p concession,' one pensioner, unfamiliar with the changes, told the driver. 'What is your destination?' he demanded. 'I don't know what you mean,' she replied. 'Faur are ye ga'in?' he then asked. 'I'm ga'in to my daughter's for my dinner!'

DEPT of Where-were-you-when-Kennedy-was-shot. We hear of a quine in Furryboots City who

remembers very well. She was visiting her mother shortly after news of the assassination broke. 'Isn't it terrible, mother? Kennedy's been shot,' she said. 'Oh dear, poor Calum,' replied mother, who clearly had not been watching the TV news bulletins.

AN aged Glasgow beggar approached two youths with a request for alms. The teenagers, hardmen in the making, replied (oaths deleted): 'No way, you'll jist huv tae go oot and steal like the rest o' us.'

A MEMBER of Hamilton Golf Club wrote to let us know that one of the dress rules there stipulates 'No jogging bottoms'. He added: 'My wife has taken this personally and refuses to go.'

DEPT of Nicknames: Two of the top cops in the Greenock division of Strathclyde police station are known as Cockbridge and Tomintoul because, it is alleged, people often encounter great difficulty getting through to them.

ACE Services of Partick, which does window cleaning, glazing, paintwork, and a bit of plumbing, set themselves apart from more ordinary tradesmen by describing themselves as 'rebel workmen to the bold and the beautiful, the proud and the passionate'. As an added inducement to these beautiful, passionate customers, Ace offers a free five-minute guitar lesson every time they get their windows cleaned.

A SOUNDBITE from the Celtic Film and Television Festival in Londonderry. A Belfast TV producer was pontificating with such phrases as 'the problems of going through the proscenium arch of television' and 'TV just eats up performance'.

A more down-to-earth chap in the company observed: 'To hear

him now, you'd never guess he started his career in a furry suit as one of Mike Batt's Wombles.'

From the same fount of wisdom: What is the collective noun for TV producers? A crock.

TWO literary views of Scotland. First, a novel called *Scottish Ecstasy* by one Rebecca Sinclair. It is published by an American firm, Zebra Books, in its Lovegram Historical series. It is a tale of everyday life in Scotland, as can be seen from the following blurb: 'Scottish beauty Vanessa Forster had offered herself as pledge to the superbly-muscled Alasdair "The Devil" Gray until Clan Forster could pay the fine they owed him. But the emerald-eyed chit of a girl did not anticipate that her duties as pledge included warming The Devil's bed.'

Slightly closer to reality is the description of a new book about life on the island of Arran: '*On Arran* is an absorbing account of island life . . . everything from visitor attractions to septic tanks and sewage – a must for every local and a quick dip into Arran affairs for the visitor.'

A FINANCIAL institution decided to send a mailshot to its wealthier clients. The computer was duly instructed to select appropriate customers. The computer expert then tested the program with an imaginary

customer called Rich Bastard. As was bound to happen, 2000 esteemed clients received letters with the greeting: 'Dear Rich Bastard'. The luckless programmer was subsequently sacked.

FOR those who cannot even boil an egg, we recommend the cookbook published by St Ninian's Church Women's Guild of Stonehouse, Lanarkshire. The ingredients for Kay Nichol's failsafe recipe are: 'One or more eggs, the Methodist Hymn Book and a pan of boiling water.' The method is simplicity itself: for a hard-boiled egg, sing all verses of 'Onward, Christian Soldiers'; for medium-boiled omit one verse, and for soft-boiled sing only two verses.

CLYDEBANK Crime Prevention Panel informed visitors to the local police station open day that a 'light finger buffet' would be provided after the event.

THE parish bulletin of St Gabriel's Church in Glasgow contained an item thanking parishioners for making donations to an organisation called Play In School Hospitals. It then informed the readers that 'PISH is now in the happy position of being centrally funded.'

BBC Scotland head of television Colin Cameron was at the Oscar ceremony where the BBC-sponsored *Franz Kafka's It's a Wonderful Life* short film won an award. Cameron was in full Highland dress for the occasion and was approached by an impressed member of the audience with the words: 'I've been at the Oscars for the past 15 years and this is the first time I've seen anyone wearing the quilt.'

A DIALOGUE on the bus from Glasgow Airport to Buchanan Street: An American tourist was greatly concerned that the driver had set off without checking the bus boot was securely closed and was complaining that her luggage was going to end up strewn over the road. 'Listen, hen,' said the driver. 'I'm like Sherlock Holmes – I've never lost a case yet.'

We know what he means, but shouldn't that be Perry Mason?

DIARY readers' appetite for Scottifying Hollywood movies remains undiminished. Stewart Smith from Hamilton tells us that locally *Four Weddings and a Funeral* has been retitled *Five Co-op Purveys*.

A GALLIMAUFRY OF WEE STORIES

THE East Ayrshire Council headquarters in Kilmarnock boasts not one but two rooms with padded walls and two-way mirrors. Nothing to do with the expected behaviour of the elected members of East Ayrshire, we are told. The building used to be a secondary school which was equipped with the rooms to deal with difficult and unruly pupils who needed to be calmed down in times of severe stress. But you never know when these facilities might come in handy.

HEATHER Major, a teacher in Dunfermline, asked some second-year girls if they could tell her what Impressionism was. 'It's French for colouring-in,' one replied.

ON the O.J. Simpson front, we heard his lawyers are so good even he believes he is innocent.

An unreported exchange between O.J. and his lawyers:

'There's good news and bad news. Bad news, they've definitely identified the blood at the murder scene as belonging to you. Good news, your cholesterol level is really low.'

THE power of language and the way it can break down frontiers. Or not, as the case may be.

A woman from Carfin was on a pilgrimage to Lourdes and wanted

to take back a memento of her visit. She was having terrible trouble making herself understood and was relieved to find a little souvenir shop with the sign 'English spoken here' prominently displayed in the window. The woman carefully selected her preferred religious artefact, a statue of Mary and the baby Jesus, and approached the girl asking: 'Excuse me, hen, whit does the likes of this run in at?'

A VISITOR from the United States was extolling the virtues of all things Scottish after returning to the home of the brave and the land of the free. She waxed lyrical in particular about the treatment she had received at Glasgow Airport from all of the staff both on the ground and on the Loganair plane aboard which she was bound for the islands. The plane was the rather Transit van-like but very functional Shorts 360. Our friend wrote a wee note to those at the airport who had treated her so well: 'We were taken on board and headed out towards the runway. It was all very comfortable, but imagine my surprise when what I thought was the airport bus taking us out to the airplane suddenly picked up speed and took off.'

A PAISLEY printing company used a half-page advert to admit: 'Greenlaw Graphics has been in business for 11 years and during that time we have pleased and displeased our customers, not been paid for jobs, lied to, been cheated and conned, suffered problems with the tax department, been flooded, broken into on many occasions, been forced to move premises, had power cuts, deliveries of incorrect stock, and printed jobs in the wrong colour.

It isn't easy, and the only reason we're in business is to see what happens next. Pop in and see us. At least the coffee's good.'

WE don't know what the Duchess of Kent must think about the familiarity of Scottish men. She was up on royal duty at the Tennents Scottish Cup final and had to go through the ordeal at the pre-match presentation of being kissed by all the Airdrie team. Then, just after she resumed her seat in the directors' box, a fan passed his programme over several rows of seats to the duchess with a piece of mime which indicated that he wished her autograph. This sort of thing is normally frowned upon on royal occasions but the delightful duchess was happy to reach into her royal handbag for the royal pen and append the royal signature. The programme was duly handed back, only for the chap to shout out that it was actually her phone number he was after.

A SHOW at the Collective Gallery in Edinburgh offered: 'Installations using vestments, sheets and blankets, carbolic soap, soot, lace, wax, wire wool and engine oil, explore Patricia Mackinnon-Day's experiences as a Catholic child in the Glasgow tenements of the 1960s.' See being a Catholic in a Glasgow tenement? See engine oil?

DANIEL Conlan from Maryhill wrote: 'You think you were poor. We got a hard-boiled egg to decorate at Easter. When we went to the park to roll the egg, my mother gave us matchboxes with instructions to collect all our bits of egg shell and put them in it. Then at Christmas time we got the matchbox back as a jigsaw.'

FROM a job application form submitted by a BA (Hons) graduate of a leading Scottish university to a leading local authority (the names of which have been deleted to protect the bewildered). Asked to describe experience gained in present post he replied: 'Employers want robots not people.' Under experience gained in previous post we find: 'All bosses are bastards.' And finally, asked his experience of unpaid voluntary activities, he replied: 'Never work for anything but money.' He didn't get an interview.

A BURNS Supper tale from Portugal. The celebration of the bard was organised in the Algarve by Willie Wilson, a kenspeckle Helensburgh builder, who has interests over there. He had imported from the auld country sundry musicians and speakers for the occasion. Also imported, of course, was the haggis. Everything went very well. Good speeches, great neeps. Except that the

chieftain of the puddin' race was, well, a bit squidgy. The owner of the restaurant, who is of English extraction, admitted that she had been expecting a comment or two on the bland consistency of the haggis. It was the French chef who was to blame. When the haggis came back from being ceremonially stabbed, he disembowelled it from its genuine sheep stomach container, put it into a blender, stuffed it into a bag with a nozzle on the end, and squirted it on to the plates. Asked why he had done so, the chef replied that he had noticed on the programme that the haggis had to piped in.

THEY know how to have their tea at the European Parliament. A wee buffet was organised with dishes from all of the 15 EU nations. From Austria's offering of sachertorte to Spain's tortilla it was an extravaganza of good grub. But haud on, what is this entry on the menu under 'Angleterre – cheddar et roast beef'. Apparently, Scotland, Wales and Northern Ireland do not exist. It's enough to make your haggis curdle.

HEARD at an Ayrshire Burns Supper: 'Shoplifting has got so bad in Saltcoats that up at the chapel they've had to put in a new confessional for eight items or less.'

CRAWFORD Beveridge, chief executive of Scottish Enterprise, related how a determined inventor laid siege to their Bothwell Street offices. Encamped in the foyer, he was adamant that he had to speak to a senior director. The junior person given the task of dealing with the situation was finally able to elicit the nature of his request. The inventor had perfected a time machine and all he needed was some enterprise funding. The message was relayed upstairs and the answer came back from the director that he didn't have time to see the inventor that day. But if the inventor could come back last week, the director would have time to see him.

AS Old Labour became as distant a memory as Keir Hardie's bunnet, we noted the title of a speech made by Campbell Christie, general secretary of the Scottish TUC. The talk at Strathclyde University was on 'Trade Unions and the Challenge of the New Human Resources Management Environment'.

LISTENERS to the *Tom Morton Show* on BBC Scotland steam radio were treated to a cookery demonstration by award-winning chefette Anne Nichol of the Dunain Park Hotel in Inverness. Her dish was a smart little number – monkfish wrapped in bacon. Can you not just hear the bacon sizzling across the airwaves? No expense was spared, the BBC even buying in an electric frying pan for the occasion. Well, there was a bit of cheating. The chefette could not get any monkfish and substituted haddock. And, do you know, none of the listeners noticed. That's the wonder of cooking on the radio.

A RASH OF WEE STORIES

LABOUR MP Tommy Graham was visiting some of his Linwood constituents whose homes had been flooded. One lady by the name of Lily related that she had been rescued by some nice polis in a rowing boat. 'I'd been to the fortune-teller two weeks before and she told me I would be going on a boat trip,' Lily told him. 'But she never said the trip would be up my own street.'

CHRISTMAS greetings to Mr Watson Kerr, mine host of the Canny Man's pub in Morningside Road, Edinburgh. Mr Kerr takes a delight in exhibiting a robust attitude to what we committed topers call amateur drinkers. Mr Kerr issued a seasonal edict in defence of his regulars. He says: 'They give me their custom 365 days of the year and I'll be damned if I'll allow hordes of paper-hatted, once-a-year clowns to disrupt things here.'

The highlights of Mr Kerr's

Christmas message to his customers include: 'No office parties. This means have it elsewhere and, after it, don't be tempt ed to bring the remnants of half-drunk prats back here. They won't get served and you'll be barred.

'No Christmas decorations. This means I don't want anyone cutting down a tree on my behalf – and I'm not a friend of the earth.

'No free nips. This means nobody gets one on the house here at any time and that includes the festive period. Please do not ask.

'No festive lunch. This means be truly thankful I'm not going to serve Christmas pudding, give you

BUSINESS LUNCHES

The Heid Inn

ROAST BEEF Tuesdays OAP Thursdays

a cracker, and charge you double . . . I'm serving lunch as usual and you'll have to wait as usual and more than likely the food will be cold by the time you get it, as usual.'

Mr Kerr informed his clientele that at New Year his hostelry would not open for the bells. 'Go to the Tron to mingle with people from all walks of life,' he recommends. 'But watch out for the lighted torches on the parade,' he warns, 'and if you must drink from other people's bottle wipe it first. In the event of someone either burning you or hitting you with a bottle, the Royal Infirmary is only a few minutes away,' he adds.

And by the way, there will be a 20p surcharge on drinks on Christmas Eve, Christmas Day, New Year's Eve, New Year's Day, and Mumpers Day (2 January) to cover for staff working unsocial hours. But, as Mr Kerr concluded his missive: 'Having said all of

that, have a nice Christmas and New Year.'

PETERHEAD Prison became involved in a rather unusual test case of the rules and regulations which allow inmates to pursue their religious beliefs and practices. Colin Gilder, prisoner number 66/92, had his lawyers write to governor Alec Spencer to complain that he was not being allowed to pursue his ritual worship as a Paganist. He was particularly upset that he was not allowed a private room to meet his high priestess. Neither was he allowed to have the candles necessary for his pursuit of Odinism. Another problem, he claimed, was that he was not permitted to wear his beaded headband, apparently a compulsory bit of kit for Paganists at certain times of the year.

All this was in contravention, as you probably know, of Article 18 of the Universal Declaration of

Human Rights. In protest, Mr Gilder went on hunger strike. Mr Gilder's lawyers, the local firm of Masson and Glennie, chose for some reason to send a copy of their letter to the governor to the local newspaper, the *Buchan Observer*. This sparked off a lively correspondence from other Peterhead inmates.

The next edition of the Buchanie, as the local paper is called, carried a letter from Adam Belmonte, prisoner 66/87, under the heading 'Governor bans my Elvis Lives rituals, too!' Mr Belmonte wrote: 'The governor refuses to allow me to hold my crepe-soled rituals and hip-swivelling gyrations within the chaplaincy; nor does he acknowledge my long-standing membership of Thomas the Tank Engine Fan Club by allowing me communication with the millions of my fellow members throughout the country.

'Further, I suspect he is actively undermining my membership of the Young Conservatives by refusing me permission to hold drunken orgies during which the ceremony of raising the kilt to display my intelligence and fitness to govern is an important part.' Mr Belmonte also complained that he was denied the chance to give a lecture on the cargo cults of Polynesia.

Another Peterhead prisoner wrote to the Buchanie to point out that it was difficult to take Mr Gilder's hunger strike seriously when he was refusing food but stuffing himself with sweets and other goodies from the prison shop.

KIDS with GAS EAT FREE
1 Free Childs Meal with 10 gallon Purchase

Governor Spencer told the Diary: 'I'm tempted to say the whole thing is not worth the candle. But it is my duty to ensure that people have their religious rights.' But a pagan service in the chapel was obviously not on. Mr Gilder would be allowed to have meetings with his high priestess under supervision in the interview room. And before any readers get all heated at the concept, it should be pointed out that the said high priestess is a mature lady and it's all above board in a Paganist, Odinist sort of way.

INAPPROPRIATE music. The scene is the Glasgow housing department homeless persons unit. The clients, usually battered wives and the occasional bruised husband, were being treated to Frank Sinatra crooning 'I Get a Kick out of You'.

ARCANE is the word which springs to mind for some of the communications received at the Diary desk. Such as an extract from a publication called *Willings Press Guide* which lists the titles and details of every periodical known to man or woman. Our correspondent draws attention to a publication listed therein. It is called *Sexual and Marital Therapy*. Included in the information for those who would wish to advertise in this august journal are the words: 'Special positions: Inserts accepted.' What can it all mean?

A NAE Luck award to the youth who stole a car to facilitate a visit to his loved one in one of HM's Scottish penal establishments. He was apprehended as he made his way home. Sharp-eyed prison staff had become suspicious. As you would when you see someone starting his motor with a screwdriver.

THERE'LL Be a Welcome in the Glens: In the two-page set of instructions issued to guests staying at the Grand Hotel, Fort

cleaning linen and the replacement costs of beds. The charges raised in respect of replacement mattresses/divan bases will, upon payment, result in the relevant party becoming title holders to the destroyed fixtures and fittings. The property has to be forthwith removed from the hotel by the new proprietor as the hotel management categorically refuses to subject future guests to inferior and/or suspect sleeping facilities. The charge being £100.'

If you see a guest leaving the Grand Hotel, Fort William, with a bed on the roof rack . . . just don't ask.

William, is an item headed 'Fouled/soiled mattresses/divan bases'. It makes particularly gruesome reading, especially over breakfast: 'As all apartments have private facilities, parties guilty of "Fouling" will be charged for

SCOFF'S Brasserie at the Argyll Hotel in Sauchiehall Street, Glasgow, proclaimed: 'Kids – eat two for the price of one . . .' We are very fond of kids at the Diary but we couldn't eat a whole one, far less two.

A RAKE OF WEE STORIES

THE scene is a company dinner-dance with all the organisation's aspiring movers and shakers in attendance. One particularly earnest junior manager turns up sporting a rather natty green cummerbund. During a dance requiring much shoogling, said natty cummerbund comes undone and is revealed to be a rolled-up Subbuteo pitch.

THE scene is a film set near Fort William where Mel Gibson, the Aussie screen icon, is making his movie *Braveheart*. Mr Gibson is walking along the road chatting to another actor in the cast. They pass two local women and, as they do so, hear the words: 'Ah tell ye, it is him.' 'No, it cannae be.' 'It is. It's Jimmy Blair frae *Take the High Road*.'

Mel's companion was indeed none other than Jimmy Chisolm, obviously more famous in Fort William than any Hollywood superstar. And this despite the fact that his Jimmy Blair character had been killed off with a cerebral haemorrhage seven years previously.

A ROYAL Marine corporal who piloted a landing craft was asked for his memories of the Allied invasion of the Normandy beaches. 'They were noisy, dirty, and overcrowded. The weather was terrible and worst of all the Germans had got there first,' was his reply.

WHEN Norman Lamont, former Tory Chancellor of the Exchequer, was a pupil at Loretto, he was invited to spend the summer

39

at the home of another boy (who shall remain nameless). When asked one day by the lady of the house to choose which of the many and various young and manly outdoor pursuits he would like, young Norman inquired if it might be possible for him to stay in the kitchen and ice cakes.

THE setting is a school play at an educational establishment for young ladies. The play is based on *The Diary of Anne Frank*. The girl chosen to play Anne is, in real life, one of the snottiest and most disliked in the whole school. Thus, when we get to the scene when the Nazis burst into the house where the Franks are hiding, there is a chorus from the leading lady's classmates of 'She's in the attic!'

HIGH-TECH dentist W. Lloyd Jerome of Glasgow provides virtual-reality goggles which enable patients to watch movies during treatment sessions. Which Hollywood gems would provide the biggest distraction during the extraction? *Fatal Extraction, Top Gum, A Bridge Too Far, A Fistful of Molars, Miller's Flossing, Bill and Ted's Bogus Denture, Driller Killer, The Thomas Crown Affair,* and *Root 66.* Or *The Man with the Gold in Gum, How Clean Was my Wally?, Toothless in Seattle, The Filling of Sister George, The Teeth of Baghdad, When Sally Got Wallies,* and *The Gums of Navarone.* Or simply, *Roots.*

GERALD Carroll, a Labour councillor for Carnwadric in Strathclyde region, was re-elected despite using these words to attack the Conservatives: 'They shamelessly gerrymander to retain the occasional Tory satrap in power.' Mr Carroll tells us that the leaflet provoked not a single query on matters political but 22 inquiries asking what a satrap was.

A CAMEO from the days when Glasgow clippies ruled the city's tramcars. The tram is stappit fu', as usual. A Bearsden lady, dressed to the nines for an afternoon in town, is among the multitude being denied access. 'But I must get home to prepare my husband's tea,' she informs the clippie, who unimpressed, replies: 'If ye'd as many feathers in yer arse as ye hiv in yer hat, ye could fly hame.'

DEPT of Deeply Philosophical Questions: When a girl is presented with her first 'trainer bra', what exactly is being trained? And to do what?

AS Glasgow prepares to be a no smoking city by the year 2000, more and more areas become off limits to users of the weed. Such a place now is Exchange House at 229 George Street, according to a memo circulated in the council's

town clerk's office. The memo adds helpfully: 'Staff can, however, use the smoking room on the 3rd floor, 231 George Street (opposite the lift, next door to Healthy City Project).'

MUSIC is thoughtfully provided in the witness rooms at Dundee Sheriff Court to soothe the nerves. Or maybe not, as the inhabitants of the witness room at the matrimonial court were yesterday treated to Bob Marley's great hit 'No Woman, No Cry' . . .

A BUSINESS consultant was called in to advise an ailing enterprise park. On arriving to carry out his survey he was greeted with a hearty 'Hullorerr!' by the receptionist. He noted the lady was wearing a rather faded Megadeth T-shirt and a pair of 'arse-in-tatters jeans' (as he put it).

She was also chewing gum.

'First impressions are very important,' he advised. 'Do yourselves a favour and give the receptionist £60 from petty cash for a new outfit.'

He returned the next week and saw that his advice had been taken. The receptionist had a brand-new Megadeth T-shirt and a new pair of jeans. With her new-found wealth, she had invested also in a baseball cap which she sported back-to-front. And she was offering chewing gum to visitors.

IN a school in darkest north Lanarkshire the weans who appear not to be too bright are known as the CRAFT children. Not because they are given handiwork to keep them busy but because, to spell out the acronym, they Can't Remember A F****** Thing.

A large quantity of rubbish was damaged beyond repair in a fire at the coup on August 5.

THE women of Irvine decided that while their men were busy at their many all-male Burns Suppers, the ladies would have their own dinner. It was called the Mary Tontie Dinner. Before you start ploughing through the annals of Burns's life to discover who this Mary was and how many bairns she had to him, we should point out that the name refers simply to a characteristic by which Irvine, and indeed Scottish, women tend to be known. As in: 'That's Jean, she's mairrit ontie Bill.'

OUR Outer Hebridean correspondent tells us of a weel-kent figure in South Uist who got a form to apply for a gun licence. He filled it in carefully and noted that he had to provide two passport-sized photographs. These he duly obtained and turned up at Lochboisdale polis station with his form and the two passport-sized photographs of the gun.

GLASGOW is not a place to treat their lordships with an overdue deference. The scene is a city hostelry on Christmas Eve where, for some reason we know not, the conversation, or even argument, turned to Neil Carmichael, long-serving Labour MP in the West End of Glasgow. What, the denizens were debating, was the title which Neil took when he was reluctantly but rightly elevated to the House of Lords? Was it Lord Carmichael of Woodside or Lord Carmichael of Kelvinside? One bright spark thought to look in the telephone book for an answer. But Neil was still listed as plain Mr

Carmichael. 'We've got the number,' said the bright spark. 'Let's phone him.'

Thus Neil found himself on the receiving end of the traditional 'Could you settle a pub argument?' question. The answer, to save further phone calls to Lord Neil, is that he is Lord Carmichael of Kelvingrove.

A NAE Luck award to Rothesay polis who, within 24 hours of warning Bute folk to be on the alert for forged Bank of England £20 notes, found themselves on the receiving end of five of the offending bills in payment for a fine.

A SHEET of handy hints on making out report cards has been circulating among Glasgow teachers. It will come in handy also for parents when trying to decipher what the teacher really wants to say about their dear children:

A BORN LEADER: Runs a protection racket.

EASY-GOING: Bone idle.

GOOD PROGRESS: If you think his or her work is bad now you should have seen it a year ago.

FRIENDLY: Never shuts up.

HELPFUL: Creep.

RELIABLE: Grasses on mates.

EXPRESSES HIMSELF CONFIDENTLY: Cheeky little bastard.

ENJOYS ALL PE ACTIVITIES: Thug.

DOES NOT ACCEPT AUTHORITY EASILY: Dad is doing time.

OFTEN APPEARS TIRED: Stays up all

night watching horror movies.

A RATHER SOLITARY CHILD: Smells or has nits.

POPULAR IN THE PLAYGROUND: Sells pornography.

A VERY INQUIRING MIND: Often caught playing doctors and nurses.

A WEST of Scotland lawyer had the task of defending an accused of the Orange persuasion. The case was continued to 12 July. The accused urgently informed his brief that he had a previous engagement on that day, namely marching in uniform through the streets of Belfast. The lawyer managed to get the date of the next appearance changed by informing the bench that his client had already booked a walking holiday in Ireland.

DEPT of We Know What They Meant. A spokesperson for the British Standards Institute commenting on changes to new improved Euro regulations for condoms: 'BSI welcomes the new standard as its requirements maintain a stiff specification, whilst still allowing flexibility for manufacturers.'

On much the same subject, we had the following extract from a recent wedding guide in the *Stirling News* to the duties of a best man: 'He should look after transport to the reception and make sure everyone has a ride.'

A SCOUR OF WEE STORIES

A NAE Luck award to the two Dunoon polis who borrowed an unmarked police car to go to England to pick up a prisoner. They returned the car, reporting no problems 'despite passing very close to a flash of lightning on the motorway'. It transpires it was in fact the flash from an English police force's speed-trap camera. The relevant photie and speeding ticket winged its way Dunoon-wards.

THE Edinburgh Festival Theatre, according to its programme, is 'working to provide deep and lasting satisfaction to all theatre-goers regardless of race, age, class, gender, or sexual orientation'. This would seem to be confirmed by the section headed High Heels: 'Edinburgh Festival Theatre welcomes theatre-goers wearing high heels. Persons may use the front-of-house lift for easy access to the Dress Circle and Upper Circle seating and cruising areas.'

And if you don't fancy cruising, there's always the theatre caff. 'Café Lucia offers the finest coffees, irresistible pastries and petit choux, luscious tarts . . .' and is described as 'a salon where passionate theatre-goers may reel in a passable pick-up, just like in the 1890s.'

UNITED Airlines offered a 'Scottish Feature' dish on its Connoisseur Class menu on flights out of Glasgow. One example was

45

'Rack of Lamb baked with a Cumin Crust and offered with a Jalapeno Rosemary Jus, Green Beans with Shiitake Mushrooms and a slice of Artichoke Potato Pie'. They eat little else in downtown Govan.

ADAM MacNaughtan, singer-songwriter and all-round folk hero, had a slight problem when Glasgow held its annual Open Doors weekend recently. He was determined to take time off from running his bookshop in Parnie Street to sample some of the city's architectural glories but could find no one to mind the shop. Thus the following notice could be seen in the window of Adam Books: 'This shop is closed for the annual Glasgow Open Doors festival.'

Dementia is not usually a subject for humour. But here goes. A document landed on our desk. It was entitled Planning for Community Dementia Services in Barking and Havering. Barking and Havering, in this context, are not symptoms but boroughs in the deep south of England. It seemed entirely appropriate that the above areas should share a health authority. And that they should be at the leading edge of dealing with dementia. To excuse this outbreak of bad taste, we quote from a note from the consultant psychiatrist who sent us a copy of the report: 'As we all know, the subject of dementia is a serious and distressing one but light relief in what can often be a distressing field to work is very welcome.'

Or, as we say in the Diary, if you're suffering from dementia, just go home and forget about it.

APROPOS of not a lot, one of our many moles at the Scottish Enterprise offices in Bothwell Street brought to our attention the names of some of the women who work there. The staff directory lists Maretta, Cerise, Sasha, Severine, Dania, Maryse, Nuala, Edel, Gini, Imelda, Tamara, Belle, Tara and Ute. And not a single Senga.

ACTOR Mel Gibson was chieftain of the Chicago Highland Games, sponsored by none other than Tennents, the lager that made Glasgow famous. As part of the publicity, the Chicagoans were urged to look out for Mel's new movie, *Braveheart*, the story of the Scottish hero 'Sir William Wallis'. Yes, that William Wallis who went on to found a chain of women's dress shops.

ONE of the more attractive freebies at the Edinburgh Television Festival was a smart briefcase handed out to delegates by Central Productions. Thus the bar and foyer of the George Hotel, where delegates foregather, were littered with identical cases. When one delegate returned home, with said piece of luggage, his wife kindly unpacked it for him. And was not best pleased to discover the briefcase contained some briefs, of a frilly feminine kind. There were other articles of an embarrassing nature. And, fortunately for the chap returned from days of earnest debate and study at the festival, a wallet containing the credit card and personal details of another distinguished delegate.

GREAT Rail Announcements of Our Time: The scene was Haymarket station, where the Glasgow to Edinburgh train had stopped but the passengers remain trapped inside.

'We would like to apologise for the late opening of the doors,' a voice announces to the pas-

47

sengers. 'This is due to the guard's incompetence. This incompetence was caused by an accident at birth, and everything possible is being done to rectify the situation.'

THE scene was a metal-working factory in Kilmarnock. An operative had suffered an accident, a cut artery in his arm was spurting blood everywhere, but the works' nurse managed to deal quickly with the situation. After administering a few stitches and a tetanus jag, she told the chap to go and rest up for an hour and come back for a check-up. He duly returned and informed the nurse that he is feeling much better but is extremely hungry. 'There is no problem about eating,' she says. 'Just have your lunch as normal.'

'I would,' he replied. 'But my mate thought I was getting carted off to hospital and he ate my piece.'

A GYNAECOLOGIST examining a patient in a Glasgow hospital was surprised to find a first-class stamp adorning the lady's bottom. Intrigued, he asked for an explanation. The lady was equally puzzled until she remembered that she had popped into a toilet which had no paper. She rummaged in her handbag and eventually found a tissue with which to dab herself. The stamp, she explained, must have been lying loose in her handbag.

THE urinals at the Grand Ole Opry country music club in Glasgow proved to be a bit of a stretch for a couple of smallish

visitors when the venue was used by Scottish TV. On inquiring of a club member why they had to reach for the sky, the short-ersed visitors were informed that the toilets were built with stack-heeled cowboy-booted guys in mind.

MAKING FREE WITH THE FRENCH

HERALD readers were invited to mark the 700th anniversary of the Auld Alliance by sharing anecdotes which reflected the Scotland–France connection and the languages which divided the nations.

MARY Kelly of Burnside wrote: 'During the Second World War, a battalion of Free French troops was stationed close to our home, a small mining village in deepest South Ayrshire. A young lady of the village, Henrietta Dalton (not her real name, she might read *The Herald*) spent much of her leisure time in the company of the French soldiers. So plenteous were her alliances that when the headmaster of the village primary school asked the senior class "Who is the leader of the Free French?" They unanimously chorused: "Henrietta Dalton".'

IAN McLaren Thomson of Bearsden told of the time he was called upon to help run a summer school in central Scotland for sundry Parisian weans. One of his tasks was to find lodgings for the female French teacher. 'In desperation I asked the obliging "*maîtresse*" of the local corner café if she could put a card in her window. To my delight she said I need look no further. She herself had a spare room. She and her husband were the nonpareil of hospitality. Mademoiselle (the French lady in question) raved about the excellent cuisine, the unstinting largesse, and the way she had been welcomed *en famille*.'

50

Everything went very well and when, some months later, Mr McLaren Thomson had occasion to pass through the town he looked in to see the lady host. Had Mademoiselle Brillard been in touch since her return to France? he asked.

'Not since my husband flew out to live with her at the end of August,' the lady replied with admirable sang-froid.

DAVE Stormonth from Paisley was working in Paris. One of his fellow Scots had a night on the town and ended up tired and confused. Could he find his hotel? Non. Thus a somewhat inebriated Scot gave himself up to the gendarmerie and confessed that he had no idea what hotel he was staying in or where it was situated. Could he perhaps give a clue, asked *les flics*.

'See that big tower thing,' he replied. 'I can see it from my hotel windae.'

JEAN Neilan of Barrhead told how a young French graduate was nearing the end of his year-long exchange in a Glasgow office. It was fair to say that his Gallic charms, particularly his delicious French accent, had not gone unnoticed by the girls in the office. They decided that a parting gift was in order. The man was asked what memento he would like. He was an outdoor type and asked for a copy of the latest book by explorer Sir Ranulph Fiennes. His meaning got lost somewhere along the way and he was puzzled to receive at his presentation a copy of the Renault 5 handbook.

BILL Baillie of Cumnock recalled summer schools which brought together local pupils and their French counterparts. One of the activities was a Scotland v France football match. Mr Baillie was refereeing one such game when an Ayrshire player in midfield bawled to his goalie: 'Haw, Jock, hit it a blooter.'

At which a French boy turned to him and asked: 'M'sieu, Qu'est-ce que c'est blooter?'

CHARLES Fryars of Lauder remembered a trip to France

undertaken to improve the linguistic skills of pupils of the old St Mungo's school in Glasgow. The party were staying in a hostel in Paris where it was discovered that they were short of a mattress for the beds. The teacher in charge dispatched a spotty youth to obtain one from the concièrge. The boy returned with no mattress but a well-cuffed ear which he had earned by saying to the surprised and outraged lady: 'Madame, je voudrais un matelot, s'il vous plaît.'

JOCK Davidson of St Monans, Fife, told of a case in the Parisian equivalent of a Scottish police court. In the dock was none other than Harry McElhone, a Dundonian who went on to become famous as founder and patron of Harry's New York Bar at 5 Rue Danou in Paris (as used by Hemingway and many other celebs). Harry, being a Dundonian, had ended up on a minor charge and found himself on the receiving end of a hard time from the prosecution lawyer who was ranting on about this foreigner who had no respect for the laws of France. Harry, defending himself, pointed out that under the Auld Alliance, the French King Louis XII had in 1513 issued the decree of *Lettres de Naturalité* which bestowed on Scotsmen the same rights as Frenchmen under the law. Case dismissed.

NORMAN Brown recalled a French–Scottish summer school in Ayrshire when a geography teacher chum of his had been drafted in to help control the *jeunesse*. His eagle-eye spotted that a boy and a girl in the back seat of the bus were engaged in osculatory activity in a rather too obvious attempt to promote the Auld Alliance. Being rather proud of his command of French, he thundered: 'Défense de baiser dans l'autobus.'

This produced hysterical laughter from all the French boys and girls on the bus. The teacher was not to know that the verb 'baiser', since he had learnt it, had moved on and as well as meaning to kiss had assumed a much coarser meaning, a word starting with the letter F and involving asterisks.

GEORGE Gorman of East Kilbride had some memories of the Free French troops who were billeted in Johnstone during the Second World War. The soldiers had learned most of their English from the local factory girls. A French officer was one day sitting on the long seat at the back of a bus. He was dressed smartly in uniform and looked every inch the perfect gentleman. Indeed, when a lady boarded the bus at a subsequent stop, the Frenchman gallantly stood up and offered her his seat. The overall effect was somewhat spoiled by the words with which he accompanied his gesture. He stood up, clicked his heels, saluted, and said with all the natural gallantry of his nation: 'Madame, plank your arse down there!'

MARGARET Glenday from Monifieth told of a Scots lady exercising her French on holiday. Having thoroughly enjoyed a gâteau recommended by *Monsieur le patissier* she decided to order another one 'aussi grand que ma derrière'.

ROBERT McIntyre of Greenock was on holiday in France *en famille*, complete with mother-in-law. One hot and humid day they were sitting on a train in the Gare St Lazaire. A chic and sophisticated French lady boarded the train and sat beside the mother-in-law. The French lady proceeded to fan herself with her glove, at which point mother-in-law leant forward, patted her on the knee and asked in concerned tones: 'Are ye a' puffed oot, hen?'

ALISTAIR Donald of Langholm told of a Glasgow businessman, extremely wealthy but a bit of a rough diamond. Informality was his keynote which did not go down too well with some of the staff at his bank, a Glasgow branch of one of the Scottish clearing houses. One day the teller was extremely snooty about the crumpled state of the banknotes our man had produced from various pockets. Dirty money was as good as clean money, our man retorted and instructed the teller to close his account forthwith, if not sooner.

He was telling his story to his pals in the pub and informed them: 'Ah jist walked across the street and went in tae yon Credit Lyonnaise and ah huv hud nae bother since. And ye know whit? Ah took the burd tae Paris last weekend and there's hunners o' thae Credit Lee-oan-ezzes and I didnae see wan Clydesdale bank.'

WILLIAM Smith of Langside recalled when he was drafted in as a translator at a council function some years ago in darkest Falkirk on the occasion of a visit by a dignitary from their French twin-

daughter. One year, travelling through Calais *en route* to Lille, the couple were enthusing as usual, remarking on how everything was prettier and more special than it was back home, how the air was cleaner, the food more delectable and so on, while daughter sat in back, silent. Suddenly, the stretch of road they travelled was filled with the pungent aroma of ham.

'Wow!' exclaimed Maw and Paw. 'Just smell that! Delicious! Oh, you know you're in France now. You don't get smells like that back home, do you?'

A few miles farther along the road, the scent was still strongly with them. Inhaling deeply and rapturing over the fact that this area must surely specialise in ham-curing, the parents were interrupted by the daughter in the back seat who said that the delicious aroma may have something to do with the fact that she had been eating a packet of smokey bacon flavour crisps.

town. The translation of the welcoming speech was going quite well until the visitor interrupted with the words: 'Dinnae bother. Ah wis in a prisoner o' war camp wi' a bunch o' Cameronians and ah learnt hoo tae speak English frae them. An' onywey, in Europe we're a' Jock Tamson's bairns.'

BETTY Shedden of Elderslie wrote with a cautionary tale of being too much of a Francophile. The Sheddens were wont, during their many motoring trips around the French countryside, to sing loudly and frequently the praises of *la belle France*. Much to the boredom of their younger

JOHN Quinn of Lenzie reported a young French person's predicament in the Ayrshire hamlet of Stevenston. Jean-Paul, an exchange student out on a day trip to Largs somehow found himself alone in the unmanned Stevenston railway station. The place was deserted and without time-tables or destination boards, so the student went to find help.

Immediately outside the station there stood a bus shelter, complete with wee local wumman and three weans. 'Excuse me, Madame,' asked Jean-Paul in his strong French accent, 'can I get a train from here to Largs?'

The woman eyed him suspiciously and, drawing her weans to her skirt, replied: 'Son, this is a bus stoap!'

THE scene is the Glencairn lounge bar in downtown Dumbarton where the denizens are watching an Old Firm football match on TV.

Also present is Jean-Louis, a young French student teacher who has had the great good fortune to be posted to Dumbarton for a year. Jean-Louis has been listening intently to the oaths and exclamations of a group of Celtic fans and confesses to being somewhat confused. 'I do not understand,' says Jean-Louis. 'This word you say all the time. "Foxy". What is this foxy?'

It was duly explained that it was not one word but three words which had been elided. The first word was 'for' and the last 'sake'.

APOCRYPHA

THE scene is a job interview involving an enthusiastic engineer at an unnamed shipyard in Northern Ireland. The interview goes roughly along these lines:

PERSONNEL: And your qualifications are . . ?

ENGINEER: Well, I'm an honours graduate. I spent two years working on the mainland, then five in America with a leading aircraft company, where I controlled experimental projects. But I've decided I want to come home.

PERSONNEL: Excellent, excellent. Now what school did you go to?

ENGINEER: Look, I'll have no truck with that. I know what you're up to. But my . . .

PERSONNEL: Please, please, I understand. It's not what you think. It's simply for the records, and for an equal opportunity programme, actually landed on us at American insistence.

ENGINEER: That's all right. This 'what school did you go to' business was one of the reasons I left in the first place. As it happens my father is a Catholic and my mother Protestant. But I was brought up in a strictly secular manner.

PERSONNEL: Of course, of course. Anything else?

ENGINEER: I would like to add that I've specialised in engine design and fuel-saving concepts. And I'm sure I could be an asset in this capacity.

PERSONNEL: Well, everything seems in order. Can your mum start on Monday?

SCOTTISH TV had a word quiz programme called *Now You See It* in which the contestants were pupils up to third year in secondary school. In order to put the weans at ease and give the audience an insight into their lives, quiz-master Fred Macaulay would ask the contestants about their hopes and aspirations. One young fellow informed Uncle

56

Fred his ambition was to be breast-fed by Pamela Anderson.

IN a police station somewhere in Glasgow, a lady copper is clearing out her desk in order to move on to greener, or even bluer, pastures. She discovers an undeveloped roll of film. She takes said roll of film to a photo shop. She returns two days later.

'I'm sorry,' says the photo shop person. 'We cannot develop your film.' 'Why ever not?' says the lady cop, wondering what on earth could be on this film. And maybe even rehearsing an alibi along the lines of it isn't really my film, I only found it at the back of a drawer in a desk at work. It could be anybody's really.

'The main reason we cannot develop your roll of film is because it is a pencil sharpener,' the photo shop person explains.

A STORY concerning a lady of honest farming stock and her six-year-old grandson who is not destined to work on the land and is indeed attending a posh Glasgow school. Calling the wee lad into the kitchen for some tea, Granny said: 'Come awa ben.' To receive the reply: 'I'm not Ben. I'm Graham.'

A PIECE of dialogue from a social security office in the East End of Glasgow where a single parent is being quizzed on behalf of the Child Support Agency as to who is the father of her new-born baby.

'Listen,' she replies. 'When ye eat a tin o' beans ye don't know which wan made ye fart.'

THE scene is a rainforest in Bali. A traveller from Glasgow is trudging along a jungle track. (A hint that he might be Glaswegian is that he is wearing a Rangers top.) He is a bit tired of walking and is heartened when he hears the sound of an approaching vehicle. Unfortunately it is going in the opposite direction. His disappointment turns to amaze-

ment when he sees that the driver is wearing a Celtic shirt. Our man is still contemplating the odds on a Rangers top meeting a Celtic one on a wee jungle track in Bali when he sees the Land Rover reverse towards him. Great, he thinks – a lift. And a chance to knock down some sectarian barriers in the unusual setting of a paradise island. The driver slows to a crawl, winds down the window, extends his middle finger, and shouts 'Get it up ye, ya Orange bastard!' before driving off.

IN an Irvine building society a chap was asked to return with proof of his identity. He went home and was now back with his mother. The assistant explained that what they really had in mind was a driving licence, passport, or something similar. 'It's a sad day when ye cannae get your ma tae identify ye,' quoth the unhappy Ayrshire chap.

THE scene is a pub somewhere in England. A Scottish visitor is enjoined to try one of the delicious sandwiches on offer with the words: 'The barman made them himself, didn't you, Marcel?' The visitor had already noticed that the barman had a gruff Scottish accent and was intrigued that he should have the name Marcel. A spot of investigation revealed that the barman was actually called Jim. But when asked by the customer who had made the sandwiches, he had replied: 'Me, masel.'

A TRUE story, honest, from a legal practice in a rural fastness of Scotland which we will not identify, for obvious reasons. A customer wrote to express satisfaction with the service which had been provided. Settlement of the account would be gladly made but (and how is this for a variation on the old cheque is in the post theme?): 'I have forgotten my signature. Could you please wait until I ask the bank to send me the specimen of my signature.'

A TALE from a Hearts supporter who took his wife along to a match at Tynecastle. She is keen but not well-versed in football matters. The

Jambos are losing 3–1 with two minutes to go. She leaps to her feet and shouts: 'Come on, Hearts, give us an equaliser.' The embarrassed husband digs her in the ribs and points out where she has got it wrong. The wife gets to her feet again and shouts: 'Come on, Hearts, give us two equalisers!'

THE scene is Easterhouse, where the building site of a new sports facility has been subjected to extensive pilfering.

Shortly afterwards, during a visit to a household in the area, a member of one of the caring professions notices that the family has been blessed with new carpeting. Closer inspection reveals that almost the entire floor area of the house, and a wall or two, is covered in Astroturf. Very hard-wearing, points out the proud tenant, and an ideal playing surface for the weans.

THE now sadly deceased local government area of Monklands, consisting as it did of green Coatbridge and considerably less green Airdrie, was a hotbed of rumour about religious bias. Even the Knights of St Columba, the Catholic men's organisation who are not at all secret, became involved. The scene is a hostelry somewhere in the aforementioned bailiwick of Monklands. The weather is appalling and a local enters with the rain running out of him, as they say. 'Filthy night,' he remarks to the only other customer in the pub. 'Masonic bastard,' is the immediate reply.

TWO chaps, from Partick and Saltcoats respectively, are on a holiday in Australia and are driving through the outback when their car is in collision with a kangaroo. They stop and find the kangaroo lying lifeless by the roadside. They prod it a bit but there is no sign of recovery. At this point (and it is because of the next bit that they wish to remain anonymous) they prop the kangaroo against the car and proceed to take some photo-

simple Barvas man who goes to the teeming metropolis that is Stornoway for a spot of shopping. Entering a shop and walking past an enormous display of footwear, he approaches the counter and inquires of the shopkeeper: 'Do you have any shoes?' The shopkeeper indicates that indeed he does. 'Give me two,' says the Barvas man.

A GLASGOW man who had steadfastly refused to buy a television licence, was caught when the detector van came to his area. The head detector, obviously in a kindly mood, said that he wouldn't prosecute the man if he went out and bought a licence immediately. He warned that he would return the next week to inspect it.

The following week the chap is on his way out when he meets the detector man in the close. He tells him he has indeed bought a licence. His father is in the flat and will show it to him. 'Tell him its behind the clock on the mantelpiece,' he says.

The detector man goes to the door and explains to the old man that he wants to see the television licence which is behind the clock on the mantelpiece. The father is astounded. 'That's some detector van you've got there,' he says.

A SCOTTISH sailor leaving the Waterloo Bar in Auckland, New

graphs. One of the chaps goes even further and dresses the unfortunate kangaroo in his denim jacket to take some more snaps. At this point the kangaroo comes to life and realises, even in its dazed state, that these two lunatics are people well worth avoiding. The kangaroo bounces off at great speed into the Bush, still wearing the denim jacket with the chap's wallet, traveller's cheques, and other important documents in the pockets.

Full marks to American Express who replaced the traveller's cheques once they had stopped laughing at the details of their disappearance.

THIS tale from Lewis concerns a

Zealand, is knocked down by a car as he tries to weave his way across the road. He is not seriously injured but his carry-out has been fatally smashed. The driver of the car is very angry. He shouts to the Gael: 'There's a zebra crossing 50 yards up the road!' To which our man replies: 'Well, I hope the zebra is having better luck than I am.'

TWO students at Heriot-Watt University in Edinburgh were candidates for a prestigious year's work-experience with a Dutch pharmaceutical company. The two could not be separated on academic grounds or other criteria. The suggested solution from the yoonie was that they both write an essay on what benefits they hoped to reap from the experience. The two lads, not wishing to see the university term go into extra-time with such an assignment, offered a quicker way. They went to the sports ground and had a penalty shoot-out to decide.

AN American couple are settling into their none-too-salubrious hotel room in Aberdeen. The chap is soon on the phone to reception pointing out that there appears to be no air-conditioning in his room. 'Well,' says the night porter, 'If it's too warm open a window. If it's too cold, just fart.'

A STORY which illustrates how increasingly difficult it is for old codgers to cope with the spread of technology. A 75-year-old chap has to renew his passport and is told there is a machine at the local supermarket where he can have the necesary photographs taken. He makes his way there, spots the booth, goes in, and sits down. He puts his money in the slot and is quite pleased at how simple it has been so far. He composes himself as he waits for the series of flashes but finds that he is watching a video cartoon of *Postman Pat*.

BAWDILY FUNCTIONS

THIS story was stolen from Dr Alex Dowers, a Glasgow GP, who collects examples of the interesting ways patients describe their ailments. He quotes the case of the mother who took her two-year-old son along to the clinic to have an abscess dealt with. When asked to describe the location of said abscess she paused to consider her words before replying: 'It's halfway between his arsehole and his wee thruster . . .'

AN Ayr lady has to attend her doctor for a routine smear test. After showering, the lady decided to apply some female deodorant from her daughter's vast collection of fragrant unguents and applications. She was mystified when her doctor smiled and said he wished more of his patients had her sense of humour. She was too embarrassed to ask what he meant and somewhat shocked to discover later that the spray she had borrowed from her daughter was in fact glitter for use at a forthcoming party.

THE scene was the Bail Appeal Court in Edinburgh where advocate Alan Muir was trying to persuade Lord 'Tiger' Morrison that his client should be freed pending trial. A major plank of the appeal was that Mr Muir's client had a severe medical problem. 'Give me details,' said His Lordship.

'Actually he suffers from chronic diarrhoea,' said Mr Muir. 'And I should point out that his application for bail is wholeheartedly supported by his cell mates.' Bail was granted.

MUSIC to be heard in the waiting room of a Glasgow family planning clinic included 'Move Over Darling', 'The Power of Love', and 'Voulez-vous Couchez Avec Moi Ce Soir'.

This story prompted a reader to relate his musical experience in a

THIS story about a medical phone-in carried on one of our many radio stations cannot possibly be true. A lady is on the line to discuss a serious problem with incontinence. 'Where are you ringing from?' asks the presenter. 'The waist down,' she replies.

DR James Campbell, a member of the Pibroch Society, is a most ingenious piper. In an article in *Piping Times*, Dr Campbell gave many fascinating hints on how to make perfectly functional bag-pipes out of unusual bits of waste material. Blue Peter has not got a look in. He has made chanters out of old broom handles and chanter reeds out of bits of plastic lemonade bottles. But it is in coping with ill-health and its effects on his piping that Dr Campbell is at his most inventive.

A foot-operated bellows he salvaged from an inflatable boat can be attached to a chanter or a small set of pipes.

'Piping friends who have borrowed these bellows have found them useful during their convalescence from abdominal operations, ruptures, and other infirmities.'

Dr Campbell recalled the time he was flat on his back in hospital on traction treatment for a disc injury. 'It was boring so I borrowed some rubber tubing from the house surgeon and used this tube to take oxygen from the

west of Scotland hospice. The family were gathered round father's bed as he endured the painful last hours of his life. As they held his hand and prayed for an end to his suffering, a hospice volunteer walked by whistling 'Please Release Me, Let Me Go'.

MORE music, this time from the genito-urinary deparment (the clap clinic, to you) of a Glasgow hospital: 'What Have I Done to Deserve This' by the Pet Shop Boys.

tap behind my bed to play my chanter. Matron caught me at it and she was not amused because oxygen is expensive.'

Even more medical is Dr Campbell's tale of turning an infirmity to his piping advantage. 'I lost my bladder several years ago and have since then, courtesy of the National Health Service, had plastic appliances for my personal plumbing. The night bag has a built-in valve so if used for air instead of fluid it makes a useful bag for the practice chanter.'

THE proprietary medicine Nytol is described as a 'night time sleep aid'. The packet also bears the words: 'Warning: May cause drowsiness'.

IN a not very PC but very direct comment on the subject of Aids, TV character Alf Garnett said:

'What they ought to do with all these Aids people, they ought to put a health warning on their bums, like on a cigarette packet – "Health Warning: This is an exit not an entrance.".'

AN Austrian company has developed the musical condom. We are not entirely sure how this bit of kit works but apparently it supplies a tune as a backdrop to the amorous activities. It surely cannot be long before a Scottish version is brought on to the market. There is no shortage of appropriate Scottish songs: 'Stop your Tickling Jock'; 'It's Nice to Get up in the Morning'; and 'The Cock o' the North'.

READERS may wish to defer reading of this item until well after breakfast since it deals with the subject of diarrhoea.

The Goanese authorities, with

the help of the University of Texas, have been conducting surveys among tourists as to how their visit was affected by this condition. The list of 25 questions asks visitors to go into great detail about any attack they may have suffered. A flavour, so to speak, can be gained from question 11 which asks: 'While you had diarrhoea, how was the stool consistency?' Answers include, 'watery (can be poured)' and 'soft (takes shape of container)'.

Question 20 is a curious one: 'Expressed in monetary terms what value would you place on a day in Goa without diarrhoea problems?'

We didn't know the dreaded condition was optional.

HEALTH hazard. A chap who has suffered a heart attack was lying in the cardiac arrest unit at the Royal Alexandra Hospital in Paisley. It was the early hours of the morning and he was slightly drugged. He was watching his heartbeat on the monitor when suddenly the line went flat. He worked out that he was still alive, he thought, but was naturally somewhat concerned about the reading on the monitor. At which point a member of staff turned up, looked at the patient, and said: 'Don't worry. You've got the one that's broke.'

Footnote: After this story appeared, the unit was given cash for a total refurbishment and the Diary was asked along to declare the new unit open.

ASK any health service administrator and they will tell you that the trouble with hospitals is all these patients who keep turning up expecting treatment. This philosophy was put down in black and white in a report on operating theatre facilities at Stobhill Hospital in Glasgow. The review referred to something called the CEPOD Report (Confidential Enquiry Into Peri-Operative Deaths).

'This report also recommended that when possible emergency surgery is best carried out during

65

normal working hours,' the Stobhill survey stated. 'From 8 a.m. to 5 p.m., Monday to Friday, emergency access to theatres is somewhat restricted. Although a designated theatre is available, there are a number of occasions when it is not staffed. This results in staff being pulled from elective sessions to facilitate emergency surgery, often causing major disruption.'

Other areas of behaviour which the Diary believed to be causing concern to hospital administrators included:

* In-patients treating wards 'like hotels'. Some of them expect three meals a day and do they ever think of bringing in their own clean sheets? No.

* Many doctors, including some consultants who should know better, are consistently failing to salute as they pass Unit Managers.

* Ambulance drivers repeatedly parking their vehicles at the entrances to casualty units without getting the appropriate ticket from the pay and display machine.

* Visitors 'skipping in' to see patients without paying the entrance fee.

IF IT'S ANY CONSOLATION
TO THE CARE-WORN REPORTER
IN SANDALS . . .

A SCRUM of journalists laid siege to the Bearsden home of Brian MacKinnon who had become famous as a 32-year-old who used the false identity of Brandon Lee to go back to school. The tenacity of the media was matched only by their ingenuity in trying to persuade Mr MacKinnon and/or his mother May to tell their story.

A combination of fierce Scottish newspaper circulation wars and 'Brandon Lee's second schooldays' being the only story in town led to the MacKinnons receiving a daily barrage of letters and notes from journalists whose only concern, honestly, was to put across the true facts. The entire dossier of written offers to MacKinnon and his mother was passed on to the Diary.

The most direct and blunt approach came from the *Daily Record* who wrote to Mr MacKinnon that they would be 'prepared to pay £20,000 for full interview and background with you on your experiences and life'. A previous approach to Mrs MacKinnon from a *Record* reporter had this more colourful message on the back of a visiting card: 'No newspaper tricks, no offers of money, or paradise hols to Hawaii. Just the plain and simple, straight-talking truth, so by the weekend this story will only be used to wrap fish and chips and you can get on with your life in peace.'

The *Sunday Post* tried a couthy approach with a letter from a lady called Barbara Bruce: 'I know you've had a difficult week and the way the press has been pestering you must have made things worse. As a mother myself I think I can understand a little of what you've been going through.'

The local newspaper, the *Milngavie & Bearsden Herald* were equally concerned in their letter to Mrs MacKinnon: 'I hope you are feeling better and managed to get

a good night's sleep. Things always look worse than they really are. I am thinking of you and if you want any help on how to handle this situation, please give me a call.'

The *Daily Mirror*, a journal well known for its sensitive exploration of how we live our lives, wrote: 'Dear Brandon, Your unprecedented and unusually spirited and original approach to life has caught the imagination of generations who dream of a return to past vistas of dreams and aspirations unfulfilled or missed. There is very little actual concrete condemnation of your amazing life-experiment. Yet there is enormous appetite to learn of the empirical results you have discovered by effectively living a life over twice.' The *Mirror* offered to 'match five-figure sums' to

explore this whole concept through Brandon's eyes.

The Sun, as you might expect, were much more to the point. A calling card was popped through the door with this message on the back: 'Dear Mrs MacKinnon, Please give me a call about Brian. It will be worth his while.' When this approach did not work, a more thoughtful letter arrived from *The Sun*: 'In order to ease the intolerable pressure you are under, which no one wants, I would ask you to reconsider our offer of £10,000 to speak to Brian. I can promise if you speak to me and tell me your side of the story you'll be left in peace. After all, Brian hasn't done anything illegal – in fact, a lot of us have an admiration for what he achieved. PS – I am blonde woman outside in red car. If you want to speak –

and it won't take long – flash the living room light off and on twice and I'll come up.'

The man from the Press Association news agency wrote: 'Have a word with me and the press pack will go home. PA News can put out any statement from you to all press and radio. I'm the care-worn reporter in sandals and blue coat.'

Many of the notes were scribbled on pages torn out of reporters' notebooks. Gordon Hay, head of bureau of the *Scotland Today* newspaper, showed a sense of humour by appending this postscript to one of his messages: 'Sorry for the quality of paper used for this missive. I had to borrow from a friend's son and you know what the cutbacks in education have led to.'

It was not only the Scottish media which beat a path to the MacKinnons' door. A BBC journalist dropped off a letter from no less distinctive a voice than Sir David Frost, inviting Brian MacKinnon to appear on his *Breakfast with Frost* programme.

This Morning, the ITV chat programme, wrote to offer the opportunity 'to put the record straight' in an interview with Richard and Judy, themselves no strangers to the unwelcome attentions of the tabloid press.

Bella magazine offered 'a substantial fee' for Brian Mac-Kinnon's story and added: 'We're a very well-respected women's magazine and would, in no way, treat the story in a sensational manner . . . I'm enclosing our current issue so you can see the sensitive way we treat issues.' The heading at the top of the *Bella* front page read: 'The bride-groom's a cheat – he slept with the bridesmaid!'

The *Daily Record* eventually upped its offer to £25,000. The *Scottish Daily Express*, in a letter to 'Mr Lee/MacKinnon', said they would beat any cash offer for the story.

The Herald eventually received a response from Brian MacKinnon as a result of a simple note offering no money but containing copies of our coverage which, we claimed, 'has been less sensational and more factual than any other paper'. Mr MacKinnon telephoned to invite *The Herald* to come to his house. And, he asked, could our reporters stop at a Chinese takeaway and buy some sweet and sour prawns and fried rice. He and his mother had been unable to get out of the house to buy food.

The takeaway was duly delivered. Brian MacKinnon insisted on paying for it.

TRADE MISSION TO CHINA

LOCAL politicians, if they have any sense, keep quiet about their wee trips around the world. Or at least make out that the sojourns abroad are arduous and absolutely no fun at all. Frances Duncan, the convener of Tayside Regional Council, took a different approach and had the council publish a small monograph entitled Convener's Trade Mission to China. Anxious that this book produced at rate-payers expense should reach a wider audience, *The Herald* Diary published a number of extracts:

THE Convener's Tale begins on Sunday, 15 January: 'On waking this morning I knew today was going to be different. Yes, I leave for a 10-day trade mission to China. First I had to check the weather. Were the roads blocked by snow (meaning a hurried change in my travelling arrangements) or would everything go to plan? All is well. I sit on my suitcase to lock it. No doubt it's been a waste of time to press and carefully pack my summer clothes. What a lovely thought – setting off for warm climes when everyone at home is shivering in the cold. My transport arrives on time and I give last-minute instructions to Ron about meals in the freezer, changing towels, undies, socks etc. He's heard it all many times over the past 24 hours!'

THE story continues in this vein and by page 2 of this ripping yarn, we have reached London Heathrow: 'Once there we have four hours before checking in for our next flight. Time hangs heavily and each member takes a turn to watch over the hand luggage while others pass the time by wandering round the airport and browsing in the duty free shops.' The narrative races on and we find ourselves on the plane with the convener: 'After dinner, followed by my favourite cup of tea, I want to reach for a

Kong on time – 2.20 p.m.' (Excuse us as we skip over the convener's stop-over in Hong Kong for a 'complete wash and change into something light and dressy'. We pick up the story as the Tayside trade mission arrives at their destination in China.)

'I make my way to the minibus along with the other members of the delegation only to be gently guided to a limousine and am joined by a number of Chinese gentlemen and suddenly a police car wails into life. The loudspeaker belted out what sounded to me like "Get off the road" or words to that effect, and cars, lorries and rickshaws ran for their lives. Woe betide anyone too slow, for the people in the police car either threw what looked like bottles or sprayed the offending vehicles.'

(On arrival at the hotel.) 'The car doors were opened by Indian Sikhs. Two more then opened the hotel door and a geisha girl pressed the lift button. Life was never like this in Tayside. All the others on the delegation had a bedroom but I had been given a suite with, by the way, two bathrooms. The management had kindly gifted me 12 red roses, a bowl of fruit, tiny biscuits, and rose petals in water. While some members headed for the bar, others, including myself, had a long leisurely bath and straight to bed.'

cigarette (it is a no-smoking flight). Ah, well, the enforced abstention can only be good for my health! By 9.30 p.m. I think it is a good idea to settle down for the night. Inside a pack supplied by the airline I find a pair of socks and ear plugs which I put to good use. I also unpack the blanket provided and blow up the neck rest I bought specially for the occasion. A film is about to start on the monitor but I decide to give it a miss. I ask for a cup of tea about 2 a.m. and with it I get a small filled roll. If I sip my tea slowly and take small bites of my roll it will help pass the time. I try to read but time is slow in passing. Life aboard begins to stir. Do I smell cooking? It must mean breakfast at 4 a.m. I have lost eight hours on the journey. It is 12 noon. We touch down at Hong

WE pick up the story on Tuesday, 17 January: 'My first duty of the

day is to be officially welcomed by the vice-governor of Hainan Province. The vice-governor and I exchanged pleasantries and gifts, all of which was screened on TV later that evening. I then visited a canning factory where coconut juice is canned. First the owner and I chatted across a table. This was followed by a tour of the factory where all the staff also live in. We move on to the engagement after lunch when the delegation are invited to view the city from a 34-storey building. When we reached the top the view was breathtaking and although a slight breeze was blowing it was quite warm, even at that height. In the evening the delegation meet with the chairman of Hainan Provincial People's Congress where again I am afforded the "head of state" position. We exchange greetings and gifts followed by a banquet in our honour and once again we were on the TV news.'

ON Wednesday, Convener Duncan manages to fit into her schedule a walk to take in some fresh air: At this point I notice I am being followed. I stop. He stops. I walk. He walks. Who is he? Why is he dogging my every step. I hurry back to the hotel and order up a cup of tea. He sits nearby. I decide to report him. After all I am alone at this time in a strange country as my colleagues are some miles away. Anything could happen to me. The person I spoke to smiles and informed me that this man was my personal bodyguard and should I require assistance at night there were another two in the bedroom across from mine.'

THE next day, Thursday, the convener gives some valuable agricultural advice to her Chinese hosts and experiences yet another example of the high-handed attitudes of the local traffic police:

'The Hainan Agriculture Science Academy are desperate for assistance from the West, particularly Tayside, to help them preserve their tropical soft fruit which is delicious. They showed a great interest in improving their cattle stock. I mentioned frozen embryos and artificial insemination but it would appear they want live calves which I suggested to them was maybe not a good idea.

'Later, "a minibus carrying a man, woman, two children, and goods overtook our entourage. With that we came to a halt. The policeman in the lead car removed the driver and placed him in the police car. We later learned that the motorist would be charged with a string of offences and have his vehicle impounded. On another occasion, a car beautifully decorated for a wedding, was also stopped by our 'friendly' policeman and stripped of its decorations. What the reason for this was I did not know.'

WE pick up the story again as the convener and fellow delegation members are treated by the vice-governor of Haikou to an 'evening of relaxation – just how relaxing I was about to discover'.

'We exchanged gifts, laughed a lot. My stories must have translated well!! During the banquet the governor asked if I was interested in Chinese medicine. "As it so happens," I replied, 'I've been troubled with my neck and shoulders for a number of years." He said: "You arrive ill – you leave well." After the banquet the entertainment begins. One of the hosts requested that Ken Macdonald and I firmly hold nine chopsticks between our fingers. The gentleman then takes a Bank of Scotland £10 note, gathers an inner strength, and "hey presto" the £10 hits the chopsticks with an almighty wallop and cuts them in half. The same gentleman looks at my neck and shoulders. He tells me I have worked hard over a long period of time and "dead blood" has gathered. He puts me into a slight trance. He then dips his finger in water on the table and throws it on my neck. I feel a burning sensation. Suddenly everyone is silent. The laughing and joking stops and blood begins to appear from six or seven different spots at the back of my neck. He then burns some paper, puts it in a wine glass and attaches the glass to the back of my neck. The blood then runs into the glass and he wipes my neck. The only mark to be seen is the one left by the rim of the glass.'

THERE is a problem as the convener fails to come out of the trance. One member thought: 'How on earth are we going to explain losing the convener in a trance when we get to Tayside!!' But all is well: 'I eventually come round feeling as if the world had been removed from my shoulders. To date I have not had a single twinge. A miracle.'

Then it was on to 'Sanya City, called the Hawaii of China': 'We are given a huge coconut each with the top sliced off and a drinking straw. The milk is very pleasant to drink and not at all as we know it in this country. Our host this evening is the Mayor of Sanya City who turns out to be a poet who has had three books of his poems published. He gifted me a signed copy of each book. He invited the delegation to join him at a karaoke in the hotel, where he

sang a song as did others. Have no fear, a number of the delegation kept the side up. Next day saw us visiting a golf course in the making. We took the opportunity to inform our hosts that Scotland is the home of golf and St Andrews is just a short distance from Tayside.'

We pick up the story at yet another banquet, this time in Sanya City: 'We discover that apart from Chinese food there are roast beef and lots of other dishes for which we have craved all week. It is only now I realise how I have missed using a fork and knife. I have become such an expert with chopsticks I can even lift peanuts!!! Our hosts have certainly given us delicacies, the likes of which none of us has seen, far less eaten. We have eaten much raw fish, particularly garoupa. The head is severed and placed before the guest of honour who is expected to eat the eyes, huge teeth, and all. Yes, it always looked me straight in the face. Funny how we appeared to get a lot of garoupa. We ate toad's chest and stomach and many other unmentionables, such as small birds, in their entirety and goose-webbed feet.'

BUT now it is time to take leave of Haikou and return to Tayside: 'Our police escort wails its way through the streets which have been cleared specially for our journey to the airport. The officers on point-duty salute. On the flight to Hong Kong I reflect on what I have seen and heard. Poverty, partially-built houses, flats and factories abandoned, poor road conditions and services, school buildings in need of repair, coconut trees everywhere, rice fields worked the same now as they were centuries ago.'

The convener pauses briefly in Hong Kong on her way home to Dundee. 'Hong Kong, Sunday: It may have been the Sabbath but it was certainly no day of rest for us. We decided not to waste the day but to see the sights and visit the famous Stanley market. Here I was able to enjoy buying clothes which were either much less expensive than at home or more unusual, and sometimes both. That evening I decided not to join the others in seeing the nightlife of Hong Kong. The previous week's activities were beginning to catch up with me and I was desperate for some "prime time" to myself.'

TUESDAY, 24 January: 'Arrived home in Tayside after 10 long days of sunshine and a hectic programme and have returned feeling grateful for the way of life which we experience here in our region.'

DEMON DRINK

ALCOHOL is a good servant but a poor master. and thankfully the source of much material for the Diary.

LAWRENCE Keith of Stranraer cited the time Dumfries and Galloway fire brigade were called to a blaze at the home of a chap renowned for his tippling. They travelled at high speed through the country roads to reach the scene but found the house well alight. They were met in the driveway by the aforementioned man of the house clutching a bottle of whisky and several glasses. He thanked the firemen for coming and invited them to have a small refreshment before they got down to work. The offer was declined by the firefighters who proceeded, with difficulty, to rescue the man's aged and infirm mother who was trapped in the upper storey of the house.

A GLASGOW man, who will

remain nameless, ended a night of over-refreshment by making a wee pillow out of his jacket. He then carefully placed his watch, glasses, and wallet beside the jacket. He lay down and fell asleep oblivious to the fact that he was at a bus stop in Hope Street.

ON the subject of sure signs of inebriation, it was confession time, on behalf of her husband, by Irene McKeown of Glasgow. Her husband had popped out for a

pint one not-too-bad summer's day, clad in jeans and short-sleeved shirt. Many, many hours later his arrival home was heralded by the dogs who had detected some activity at the front gate. Irene spent five minutes perfecting the frosty face but there was still no husband at the front door.

A quick recce of the garden revealed him to be lying sound asleep under the hedge. Efforts to awaken him by the dogs (the odd lick on the face) and the wife (the odd pummel in the ribs) both failed. Deciding against leaving him to develop hypothermia, Irene opted to drench him with a bucket of water. Being a kind soul, she even put in some hot water. The treatment worked, although not immediately. Irene had time to return indoors and watch her now relatively awake husband make his way to the front door whereupon he entered with the words: 'My God, that was some downpour.'

AN Edinburgh chap, having returned from the office party at 3 a.m., woke his wife in spectacular fashion. She came down to the kitchen to find her husband kicking the fridge. 'Why are you kicking the fridge, dear?' she inquired. 'This effan cash machine isn't working,' he replied.

ANOTHER chap who had supped well at his office party felt enough was not enough and retired to his local pub for a few hours' more drinking. Such was the extent of his cargo that, on arriving home, he walked along the hall, past his dear lady wife, to the back door. He looked out the back door, closed it, and walked back up the hall, looking into various doorways. Eventually he said to his wife: 'Excuse me. Can you tell me, where the gents' toilet is?'

FROM Stornoway, a place not unfamiliar with strong drink, we hear of a plaintive phone call from a chap asking if his doctor could make an urgent house call. The receptionist inquired, as they do, about the symptoms. 'It's just awful. My whole body is quivering. I can't keep my head still and there's this noise in my head all the time. I'm just lying here and my arms and feet are trembling.'

The symptoms passed the receptionist's test and a doctor was promised within the hour. Ten minutes later our man phoned back to cancel the doctor's visit. 'I've been on the drink for a few days and when I woke up in my armchair I didn't realise the washing machine in the next flat was on its spin-cycle.'

IT is good to see women getting involved in the art of brewing. The London Drinker Festival marked an International Women's Day by inviting some lady brewers to exhibit their products. Liz Mitchell from the Tipsy Toad Brewery in Jersey duly brought along samples of her latest beer which rejoices in the name of Black Tadger. We asked, quite nervously, the provenance of this name. It has to do with the toad part of her brewery name. In Jersey they still speak their own dialect of French. A tadpole is a tadge. The beer is a dark colour. Thus, naturally, we have the name Black Tadger. She also tells us that in Jersey French the word toad translates as *un crappo*. But we won't go into all that.

WHEN representatives of a certain double-glazing firm go on field trips to the island of Islay, they take with them in their van a number of cases of Buckfast, the tonic wine made by Devon monks and consumed in great quantities by the lower orders of the Scottish drinking-class. The Buckie is not for their own use. They swop it with the natives for bottles of the fine malt whiskies which are produced on Islay and of which, presumably, some of the locals see as an inferior bevvy to the strong, sweet red wine of the Monklands.

MENNIE'S Bar is one of the most kenspeckle howffs in Clootie City, or Dundee as it is also known. For many years it was ruled over by a barmaid called Connie. Connie is of German origin and was known in the bar for being strict in a Prussian sort of way. Her no-nonsense regime led to her being nick-named The Hun at the Till. Connie's fame spread even as far as the

Campbeltown Bar, the pub along the road, where the following piece of graffiti could be found: 'Far from the madding kraut.'

WE are not saying that Edinburgh folk are any less capable of enjoying themselves than other folk but we did notice the sign in the Pleasance Cabaret Bar. The Happy Hour, it informed us, is 9 p.m. to 10 p.m. on Monday and 'every alternate Thursday'. Let's not get carried away here happy-wise.

JIM Burke of Clarkston offered this tale of a friend called John who was courting a young lady from Lancashire. The time had come for John to go south to meet the prospective parents-in-law. He found them to be awfy nice people and it did appear that they were not entirely against the concept of him as a possible son-in-law. Until

he sloped off to the local pub where he, purely as a reaction to the stresses and strains of the familial encounter, proceeded to get blootered. So there he was, sleeping in the spare room, when he was wakened in the night by the call of nature. He attempted to make his way to the toilet, wearing nothing but a T-shirt. He got lost, of course, and found himself, in Chaucerian fashion, in the master bedroom occupied by prospective parents-in-law. The parents had been sleeping but were stirred by the noise of a 6ft 2ins and (there are no other words to describe this) hairy-arsed chap blundering about their bedroom.

John then found what he thought he was looking for. Actually he had lifted the lid of the laundry basket and relieved himself. He then crawled into the parents' bed and snuggled up to his girlfriend's mother.

FEB. 17. 1923
OCT. 25. 1986

DEVOTED FAN OF SINGER
JULIO IGLESIAS

You may be surprised to hear that the nuptials did not go ahead.

THE scene is the Glasgow–Edinburgh train where a passenger is trying to buy a refreshing but not fattening soft drink. The lady with the trolley apologised that she had no diet Coke or diet Irn-Bru. After further checking her stock she reported: 'I've got soda water but it's not slimline.'

FROM Motherwell District Court we hear of a chap on a breach of the peace charge. The fiscal put it to him that at the time of his arrest he had been in a boisterous state. 'In fact you were full of bravado,' the fiscal said. 'No,' came the reply. 'I was drinking cider and wine.'

THE Scotch Malt Whisky Society is renowned for its tasting notes. A Speyside malt was described as 'barley-sugar in cayenne . . . the nose is very sharp, but sweet and medicinal, like eating toffee while being chloroformed'. And then there was the Islay malt which we were told is 'sour and musty like an old warehouse. Watered, the spirit becomes sulphurous but classy, like aristocratic farts.'

Another whisky was described as having a nose 'like May blossom, or the air of optimism which attends marriages'. Less romantic was the analogy employed to convey the aroma of a Speyside malt: 'There is a dim mouldiness, like a gas mask left in a coal cellar. The aftertaste is curiously of worts, like being downwind of one of Edinburgh's breweries.' A dram from near Loch Lochy was said to be 'a great session whisky and therefore likely to appeal to lawyers, clergy and other hard drinkers.'

THE Washington state legislature considered a Bill making it illegal for a drunken person to buy liquor. But first representatives had to define drunkenness. Republican Dave Chappell came up with an amendment which narrowed an excess of bevvy consumption down to one or more of the following characteristics. Read them and perhaps recognise yourself:

* Being overly friendly, bragging, or talking too loudly.

* Buying rounds for strangers or the house, lighting more than one cigarette at a time, lacking the ability to light a cigarette.

* Losing train of thought (stopping in mid-sentence), slurring speech or speaking very slowly and deliberately.

* Spilling drink, missing mouth with glass.

* Arguing with employees or other customers, using foul language, appearing sullen or uncommunicative except when buying drinks.

THE DEMOTIC

THE Diary takes a deep interest in the use of the demotic, everyday language.

BILL Watson from Falkirk contributed an example which he came across when in hospital. One of the nurses was a country lass with a down-to-earth attitude. Returning from her mid-morning tea break, she would invariably exclaim before getting on with her work: 'Hauf-past ten an' no' an erse skelpt.' Mr Watson added: 'Another similar saying that comes to mind is "Half-past ten and not a whore in the house dressed."'

JACK Angus of Glasgow offered this version: 'Hauf past nine an' no' a hoor in the hoose washed an' the toffs comin' at ten.'

ROB Parker of Skye remembered it differently: 'Hauf past ten an' there's no' a dish in the hoose washed an' the toon's full o' American sailors.'

LYNDSEY Hay of the Gallowgate, Glasgow, claimed our version of this colourful phrase on the passage of time was inaccurate. The original she said, is of Liverpudlian origin and goes: 'It's 7 p.m., street full of sailors, and not a whore in the house painted.'

BILL McDougall of Bishopton recalled that in days of yore at Paisley post office, a postal inspector used to assemble his staff as soon as they had clocked on for duty at 5 a.m. and address them thus: 'Right, you lot. The day after the morn it'll be the middle o' the week and yiz huvnae done a haun's turn yet.'

BILL Maclaughlan of Kilburnie remembered his granny saying: 'Eight o'clock and no' a heid looked or a po' timmed.' 'Look at ma hair – it's like a hoor's handbag,' was another of her favourite sayings.

GEORGE MacDougall of Sandy-hills recalled: 'Eight o'clock and no' a dish washed or a heid looked.' A chap of Leith descent heard at his granny's knee: 'Eleven o'clock, not a piss-pot emptied, not a hoor dressed, and the French fleet in port.'

RHONA J. Young of Old Kilpatrick contributed a farming version from Stirlingshire where the men would be greeted of a Monday morning with: 'Hash on, boys. The day's but a blink and the rain's at Buchlyvie. The day after the morn's Wednesday and no' a stroke o' work done yet.'

JEAN Taylor of Brookfield, Johnstone brought the hale thing up to date with: 'It's 9.30 a.m. and not a fax received or a call on my mobile phone.'

WHO SAYS THE GERMANS HAVE NO SENSE OF HUMOUR?

CALL me a racial stereotyper, but I had never envisaged the Germans as a fun kind of people. Wrong, I was told. Go and observe them at karneval. I duly went to Düsseldorf to check out the karneval and have come back with the whole new stereotype that when the Germans decide to have fun they are grimly organised at so doing.

Karneval is the German pre-Lenten party, their equivalent of Rio's Mardi Gras, Spain's Carnaval, or what used to pass in these parts for Pancake Tuesday. The karneval is mostly celebrated in Germany's Catholic areas and the tradition is thought more likely to have come down from the Roman phrase carne vale, goodbye to meat for the duration of Lent.

So organised are the Germans about how to enjoy karneval that when I asked the London office of their national tourist board for information, they sent me a guidebook which was a strict set of rules on how to attend the festival. A fair example is the guidebook's injunction for Rose Monday, the day of the big karneval parade: 'Visitors should arrive in good time . . . Singing and laughter are the order of the day . . .' And don't even consider any good old Scottish queue-jumping to get a better view of the parade: 'Latecomers who think they edge their way to the front will have another think coming. Don't try it . . . You can only venture on to the roadway if

someone's keeping your place on the pavement. Don't think you can just go and stand at the front of the assembled spectators . . .'

So it turned out to be at the Düsseldorf parade. We didn't actually see the equivalent of towels on the sun-loungers but there was a definite atmosphere of order. The German tourist office actually suggested I go to Cologne which has the biggest karneval, but I was directed to Düsseldorf by informed sources who said that while the city 'only' attracted about 800,000 to its karneval, the Altstadt or old part of town provides one of the world's truly great pub crawls. Especially at karneval, when the 300 or so pubs and restaurants packed into its square kilometre get into full swing for the 'Crazy Days', as the last few days of the festival are known.

But to hark back, briefly, to the sheer organisation of the karneval. This pre-Lenten fest actually begins 'formally and punctually' at 11 minutes past 11 on the morning of the 11th of November of the year before. When, according to the brochures, the Hoppeditz (a local mad character whom I won't discuss in detail) 'moves on to the town hall and holds his moody speech to which the Lord Mayor has to respond in kind'. Then the karneval prince and princess are chosen 'at the city hall in the presence of 2500

Narren or Fools who at this time of year usually find themselves a little out of practice as regards singing, swaying and laughing'. (Sorry to keep quoting the tourist guides but I find it catches the full flavour of the event.)

There then follows months of karneval events, usually masked balls or sit-down dinners 'at which speeches often satirical and always humorous are made in rhyming couplets'. So far, so dull you might think – and all evidence that the Germans are not good at enjoying themselves. Then the karneval gets to the Crazy Days. The first such day is the Thursday before Lent, which is ladies' day. The women of Düsseldorf dress up as old market-stall biddies, complete with haggard face masks. They storm the town hall and symbolically take over the city for the day. The brazen hussies, of all ages, go around all day snipping the ends of the chaps' ties. They also drag any man who takes their fancy off for close inspection of a more straightforward symbol of manhood. It is with great sadness that I have to report arriving a day late for this part of the celebrations. Detailed conversations with two men who come up every year from south Germany to Düsseldorf karneval just to suffer such ordeals confirmed that it is an interesting night out in the old town. I cannot go into details in this family newspaper.

The guidebook, of course, has something to say on the matter: 'Let's not beat about the bush; karneval wouldn't be karneval if Cupid didn't put in an appearance. But too much spice will ruin even the best of dishes, and sexual excess is not, repeat not, the purpose of the karneval . . . Of course, given the opportunity, everyone likes to employ his or her seductive charms. But even if you sample the hors d'oeuvre at a party, remember the main dish is at home. Karneval isn't a universal love-in.'

More important than the women (really, honestly) are the wine, song, and fancy dress parades which feature on the other Crazy Days. It was good fun to watch 15 young people in grey plastic elephant suits conga through the back seats of every taxi in the old town rank. Interesting to see the denizen of an obviously gay bar dressed as a sheik, complete with ornamental knife, and truly living up to the Glasgow saying 'as bent as an Arab's dagger'. Lovely to see even the ladies beyond the first flush of youth dressing up, though at times you might wish they realised it was no longer the Thursday when they are allowed to prey on unsuspecting men.

From a Glasgow point of view, it appeared there were inordinate numbers of Partick Thistle scarves and other favours. The simple explanation is that yellow and red are the colours of Düsseldorf's immensely successful and popular ice hockey team. The colours of Fortuna, Düsseldorf's unsuccessful and consequently unpopular football team were not much in evidence. Spotted in the Konigsallee, the main street, during the parade: a chap in a Celtic FC anorak. 'You've got a brass neck wearing an outfit like that,' I said jovially. The Tim in exile growled only briefly before engaging in a conversation on the subject of, you'll never guess, 'the failings of Celtic FC'.

For the record (and, no, the photographs are not available for public consumption) I was persuaded to don fancy dress for the occasion of the big *Rosen Montag* parade. Being a last-minute job, the outfit wasn't really all that fancy. Mercedes, a newly-found German friend, produced a bright blue plastic rubbish bag for me to wear. She had kindly glued thereon a quantity of cotton wool balls which thankfully fell off in the crush. I looked extremely odd but was glad to have the chance to tell any German who would listen: 'Ich bin ein bin-liner.' It has to be said that for a parade that is about two-miles long and takes three hours to pass, the Düsseldorf event lacked any really imaginative fancy dress. Clowns, samba bands, and furry animals seemed to dominate. Whisper it, but there was even the occasional non-PC band of African natives, complete with spears.

The most common garb in the official parade was military wear of two or three centuries ago. This was interesting up to a point. The point being that each of the groups thus attired also contained sundry young women sporting the short skirts which, we had not realised, was the uniform of women soldiers of that time. Certain sections of the parade appeared to consist of hundreds of clones of Prince Charming and Dandini.

The main point of Rose Monday parade is that it is the world's biggest scramble for the weans. The guidebook assures us that 20 tons or so of sweeties are thrown from the passing floats during the parade. Having been there and seen the quantities of sweetmeats chucked at Düsseldorf's tots, that figure seems to be an underestimate. As you would expect of the German *kinder*, they were well organised for the task at hand and had brought two or three shopping bags each for the occasion. Some had formed syndicates of gatherers and bag-carriers. Others were brandishing upside-down umbrellas the easier to harvest the sweeties which were raining down upon them. Other gifts of flowers and favours were showered on the crowds. Given the amount of confectionery involved, it was appropriate that one float was also dispensing small bottles of anti-plaque mouthwash, although there was not a great deal of scrambling for these from the assembled ranks of bairns.

The parade had no shortage of music, although inevitably much of it was repetitive. The undoubted stars were the Tempo band from Holland, who managed to belt out their music as they

AMIGONE FUNERAL HOME

rode past on bicycles. This they achieved with the help of specially constructed handlebars which allowed their trombonists *et al* to pedal along and toot away to great effect. Not content with this, the band also entertained the crowd to marching-band manoeuvres while playing their tunes.

I put the Laggeri Hagger band from Basel, Switzerland, lower down on my hit list. I had seen them in almost every pub or restaurant I had visited in Düsseldorf. To use the Scottish vernacular, they could play nane. That their tuneless blastings received an enthusiastic welcome from the Düsseldorfers, I put down to good manners. The tunelessness I put down to too many beers consumed by the bandsmen. Even on the big parade it was the same cacophony. I said as much to a nearby German only for him to explain that the Basel band were playing gugga music, a form in which the art is to play wrong notes. In which case this band is simply the best.

After the parade, the music goes on in the taverns of the Altstadt. There is something for every taste with heavy rock and jazz in pubs where the '60s and '70s still live, man. I was intrigued to notice that the most popular song was 'Go West' by the Village People. But less intrigued to discover that this was a West German put-down of the Osties, the East Germans who have come west looking for but not finding the economic promised land. In the more traditional beer halls, the music can sound at times like tunes to invade Poland by. But not necessarily. On requesting translation, I found one song to be about a chap whose 'hat it has three corners. Three corners has my hat. If it has not three corners, it would not be my hat.' Go reclaim the Sudetenland inspired by those lyrics. Another song, I was informed, was all about the fact that there is no beer in Hawaii.

Ah, beer. There is beer in the Altstadt. Best of all, the alt beer, a brown concoction which is what McEwan's Export might be in a perfect world. Should you tire of the alt, try Koenig, the king of lager beers. You can tell it's good by the fact it takes the barmaid 10 minutes to pour it. The old town's pubs are fearfully busy during karneval. Organised Düsseldorfers who choose not to thrust themselves into the seething masses of merry-makers, simply organise their own alfresco pubs. Carts, prams, and specially-designed mobile structures of all sizes are pressed into service to carry kegs of beer and other essential supplies. The more sophisticated models have gantries for the schnapps, hot water for toddies, and stereo sound systems. While I'm on the subject of matters corporeally restorative, the Düsseldorf food, in such down-to-earth establishments as Schumachers, remains reasonably cheap as well as simply delicious. One serving each of the goulash soup followed by the leg of pork and roast tatties was enough for two. Even though it embarrassingly elicited an offer of an unfinished platter from the Germans at the next table who thought they had spotted a couple of impoverished Scots.

The offer of food was typical of the friendliness of the Düsseldorfers. The guidebook, of course, has something to say on this matter. 'At karneval time especially, the German is easily approachable and quick to make friends. But don't be too surprised if yesterday's bosom pal walks straight past you today without so much as a nod. Friendliness is not the same as friendship . . .' This is note entirely true. Someone I met during the festival actually waved in the railway station the next day. Yes, the Germans enjoy their karneval. If at times a little too intensely. It is definitely worth a visit but somewhat colder than Rio (take your long johns). It is safer, while Rio can apparently be dodgy. The biggest danger you are likely to face at the Düsseldorf karneval is being hit on the head with a flying chocolate bar.

ESPAÑA, SÍ

THE joys of Barcelona as a city for the young are well documented. Its nightlife is such that La Terraza club advertises: 'Arrive before five if you want to avoid the queues.' They mean 5 a.m.

The good news for those of us not getting any younger is that Barcelona is also a great place to laugh in the face of incipient decrepitude; a place where, if you can't stop the clock, you can at least make old age behave itself.

To see what I mean, check out the old fellows sitting in the sun most days on the front at Barceloneta, the city's beach area. They are in their shorts, gently tanning already impressively-bronzed paunches. They are gathered round a table, ostensibly playing cards but the main effort is going into loud debate, usually on the subject of football. With a home team like Barça they have a lot to talk about. Or the discussion could be about the lottery, politics, or something more important such as cheese or bread. One or two of the old fellows may be sipping at a coffee or a glass of red wine. Others will be pulling on the sort of cigar your average Scottish pensioner couldn't afford, even if his wife would let him smoke it.

'We come here almost every

You are warned against Solicitors, either on the property or in boats at the water's edge.

Involvement with Solicitors will be at your own risk.

day,' says Segundo Jorquera. 'Here' is the Club Atletic of Barcelona, more precisely the stretch of patioed buildings on the old front at Barceloneta which the club owns. Segundo travels across the city to the beach from his flat in the Hospitalet area, stopping off to buy some fruit, bread, and a litre carton of wine for his lunch. If Segundo wants to splash out, a number of fish restaurants in Barceloneta will provide a more than adequate three-course menu of the day for a few pounds.

How do the senior citizens of Barcelona live? Like a king, if you have a half-decent pension, says Segundo. The health service is efficient and free. You can get about cheaply on your T-4 pensioner's bus ticket. There is a network of casals, or clubs for the pensionistas with a lively social life. Segundo, at 82, still has a reputation as a bit of mover on the dance floor. He had a date with a lady friend to dance away that very evening at a casal across town. As well as the aerobic debating, the gentlemen of the Club Atletic have a wide range of sporting exercise available to them. One of the sights to behold was a chap well into the Third Age heading off across the sands clutching his wind-surfing board.

There is more to life than the material and what money cannot buy is the respect which is accorded to older people in Barcelona.

There is a scheme in the schools which brings in men and women of more than a certain age to talk to the pupils. They tell the children about local history, what life was like way back when, stories their cronies at the casals are probably tired of hearing but are new to the schoolkids. The pupils apparently enjoy the sessions as much as the old folk, who are quite happy in their role as supernumerary grandads and grannies.

The affection for and attention paid to older members of the family is replicated in society. Very often in a Barcelona restaurant you will see some old codger being spoilt rotten by barmen and waitresses.

The reader may detect in this report something of an enthusiasm for Barcelona. It is a wonderful city. Simultaneously lively and laid-back, industrious and slothful, friendly and stand-offish, raffish and prudish, bourgeois and bohemian.

A small example is a crackdown on sex shops which was announced by the Generalitat, Catalonia's autonomous government. This was no puritan backlash against the liberal excesses of post-Franco society. The Generalitat unleashed on to the sex shops not police vice squads, but trading standards officers. They were concerned the instructions and other details on the packaging of the goods on sale did not comply with local by-laws because they were not in Catalan. The trading standards officers were also checking that the various artefacts, lotions, and potions on sale met health and safety standards – another example of how they look after the older people.

Many people dream of moving to Spain to spend their later years with a bit of sun on their backs in a land where eating and drinking is a way of life. I could never imagine leaving Glasgow for good. My choice would be to apply for dual citizenship of two great cities.

A wee flat in the Gracia district near the Fontana Metro station would suit me fine. To use a Glasgow analogy, Gracia has the warmth of Partick with the style of the posher parts of the West End. It is working class but sufficiently gentrified to have some of Barcelona's liveliest restaurants, bars, and clubs.

Gracia is only three stops on the Metro from the Ramblas tourist area or a gentle hike up through the Eixample district with a chance to take in some of the best of the city's Gaudí and Domenech architecture. Being just off the tourist track the prices are lower and the people more likely to take time to have a chat, especially if you make the effort to learn a word or two of Catalan instead of Castilian.

Gracia has a young set which, in typical Barcelona fashion, puts up with the older generation. Normally, I would be found dining on *lechon* (suckling pig) at Los Caracoles or a piece of fish at Les Set Portes. My favourite resurant

in Gracia is a pizza joint. La Gavina is decorated throughout with classical Roman statues, Renaissance cherubs, and Michelangelo ceilings. It reverberates to loud rock music and serves an eclectic list of pizza toppings from caviar to black pudding. The patron, a jovial Italian, is not averse to doling out the odd free chocolate liqueur for your pudding.

Gracia is made up of narrow streets which lead to atmospheric squares. La Plaça del Diamant is probably best-known being the subject of a book and a film. But it is a run-down place these days. The nearby Plaça del Sol has become the big attraction of the Gracia with smart bars and music in the square into the small hours.

But the real heart of the Gracia is another square, slightly dowdy and the meeting place for the locals. It is called the Plaça Ruis i Taulet which, for simplicity of communication, some English-speaking residents of the Gracia refer to as the Rusty Toilet. In the Rusty Toilet, any music is more likely to be from a band of strolling players on their way home after busking on the Ramblas. The cuisine is also much simpler. The Chivito d'Oro café serves possibly the best bacon and egg roll in the world. This could well be because the roll contains fillet of pork, gammon, cheese, lettuce, and mayonnaise in addition to the egg and bacon. Then there is the side portion of *patatas bravas*, a delicious variety of chips with spicy sauce.

So how does one become a citizen of Barcelona? The Plaça Ruis i Taulet is home to the Gracia town hall, or the *Ajuntament* as they call it. After possibly too good a lunch at the Chivito d'Oro, I found myself inside the *Ajuntament* discussing with a polite, but slightly bemused, employee how to get on the Gracia housing list. Not easy since they don't appear to have any council houses.

But you can become a citizen quite easily by filling in a form and providing proof of residence. Then, in due course, you will qualify for the T-4 pensioner's bus pass to take you on the Number 17 down to the beach at Barceloneta. And the membership of the pensioners' clubs. And the Catalan language courses. And the dancing classes. You can even get a cut-price pensioner's season ticket to see Barcelona FC.

CALL me a snob but one of the great pleasures in life is arriving at the airport at Malaga, Alicante, Barcelona, or Gerona on a cheap flight and, as your fellow passengers pile into tour buses to be ferried to their mass-tourism hotels and apartments, you head in the other direction into one of these cities to get a real flavour of

Spain. Spain is currently selling itself on a theme of passion for life. I cannot speak for the Costas but in the cities there is no lack of passion, lust for life, or the movida as the Spanish call it.

Fun is a way of life especially at weekends in Spain's cities and even then they feel the need, every so often, to formalise the proposition by having a fiesta. They have fiestas because it is before Easter, because it is Easter, or because it's after Easter. Or because it's some obscure saint's day. Or because it's been a week or two since they have had a fiesta.

I arrived in Alicante for a quiet week to study the local culture, brush up my Spanish subjunctives, and perhaps sample some tapas and *vino tinto*. My fellow air charter passengers were bused off to Benidorm. I took the local bus to Alicante to find this bustling seaport heavily into celebrating the *carnaval*. *Carnaval* is like Mardi Gras, except the Pancake Tuesday celebrations lasted for a whole week. The main street was closed off and turned into a party venue. The entire population were out in fancy dress – the chaps seemed mostly to favour nuns' habits as a mode of dress, with kilts a close second. As a matter of national pride we noted the entire week was sponsored by Ballantine's whisky.

I thought the endless round of celebration quite gruelling but some of the locals felt it was a bit off that the police wanted the pubs and clubs in the old town to close early at 4 a.m. during the *carnaval*. I tried to explain to the Alacantinos the concept of the Glasgow curfew whereby the city fathers prefer to see their citizens home by midnight. They didn't understand.

IN Madrid, one of the liveliest cities in Europe, they have no concept of curfew. The night-clubs and bars go on till dawn. At least I'm told they do. I found myself exhausted by midnight just sampling the everyday pleasures of the city. By day you'll be busy drinking coffee in a terrace café of the Plaza Mayor and watching the world go by. Or admiring Picasso's *Guernica* or a Goya or two in one of the many museums and galleries. Or having a picnic in the stately Retiro park or even wider open space of the Casa de Campo.

Evenings will be spent *tasca*-hopping from bodega to tapas bar, sampling the food and drink. The Casa Abuelo, which specialises in sizzling prawns; the Museo del Jamon, a bar which is literally a museum of ham, with hundreds of varieties hanging from the rafters; the Casa Mingo, where a whole roast chicken, huge salad, goat cheese, and bottle of fizzy cider costs only a few pounds and it is so busy you almost have to fight for a table (but on no account try

BRANDING IRON
HOME OF THE
MISSION MOUNTAIN
TESTICLE FESTIVAL

to compete with the feisty Madrid matrons; give in early and graciously).

There is a bewildering choice of such places and I would have tried many more if I had not discovered the Escudero, a wonderfully old-fashioned bodega two minutes off the Gran Via main street. The Escudero sold a delicious, chilled, robust rosado wine at about 30p a glass. With each glass came a free tapas such as fried fish or *patatas bravas*. By the time you had drunk four wines you had had your tea as well. At the Escudero your entertainment was also thrown in. You could observe a wide spectrum of *madrilenos* at recreation: the old chaps energetically watching and discussing the football or the bullfights on TV; Spanish families applying themselves busily to the business of eating; the occasional transvestite – with Marilyn Monroe's bust, Madonna's clothes, and Maradona's legs.

One of the less entertaining aspects of Madrid is the pickpocket.

I was the victim of four attempts in ten days, all in the metro and all unsuccessful as the perpetrators proved themselves not quite light-fingered enough to relieve this Scotsman of his *pesetas*.

A THREE-HOUR train ride from Madrid towards the Portuguese border takes you to Salamanca. Salamanca has most of the pleasures of Madrid and Barcelona with little of their big-city crime and grime. It is an old university town, rich in history and blessed with many fine restaurants and a furious night-life. Its Plaza Mayor is truly glorious and if it is not the best square in Spain, I look forward with pleasure to seeing a better one.

It is worth turning down all the offers of free tapas for a day to save yourself for the suckling pig in the Restaurant Felix. It is also worth avoiding the nearby market, where scores of butchers' shops display the wee chaps hanging on hooks along with tray after tray of bits of animal, all of which seem to feature orifices. The Salamancan ladies were buying these orifices with great gusto but it can put off the more squeamish. Particularly off-putting was the counter featuring a large display of animal backsides. The best that can be said of this delicacy is that they are well-washed and it is quite entertaining to see how the shop assistant picks them up. Yes. Just insert a finger and lift. I cannot see this dish catching on in Scotland. 'I've got a nice pig's arse for your tea tonight, dear.'

The Salamanca students and the language scholars who make up much of the population are well served by a pub and club scene equal to any in Spain. Imagination is to the fore with clubs in many guises, such as a monastery, the Roman forum, a submarine, and a typical Spanish village street. A typical night out will begin at 10 p.m. and finish at 6 a.m. after a visit to up to half a dozen establishments. A perfect night out will start (and maybe even finish) with a visit to Las Cavas del Champan, which only sells Spanish bubbly and sells it at amazingly low prices.

Prices in the Spanish cities have caught up with, and in some cases exceeded, British levels. But it is still possible to live and eat cheaply. My perfectly comfortable hostel in Salamanca cost only £15 for a double room for a night. But

then so did two brandies in Cum Laude, the Roman forum-style disco.

THE Pamplona San Fermin festival of running with bulls is a traditional event which touches deep and resonant chords in the Iberian soul. Or maybe it's just a mixture of bravado, bragadocio, and bullshit. Larded with some good old Spanish abuse of animals.

The start of each run looks a bit like a city marathon with participants making their way through the narrow streets. The difference is that bringing up the rear are half a dozen bulls each weighing in at a thundering 1200lbs or so. The beasts are not happy about being there and are out for revenge. Another difference from a marathon is that the top honchos are to be found at the back of the pack. While the careful, fast or merely feart get out of the way, the macho men hang back to play tig with the bulls, which is the whole point of the exercise.

I can report that a three-minute head start is a fine thing in this event, especially as the running usually only lasts just over two minutes. To be entirely on the safe side it is advisable to develop a limp and duck behind a barrier when you hear the cannon announce that the bulls are loose.

The Spanish spectators tend to boo the front-runners, considering them to be wimps and a disgrace to the uniform of white trousers, shirt and red bandana. I will try to live with this, meanwhile pass this wimp his uniform of brown trousers and yellow neckerchief.

Safe behind the barrier, I saw a fellow-runner slip and fall just yards in front of a bull. Luckily for him the animal also lost its footing and merely rolled towards him. He managed to scramble to safety under the wooden fence. I had suspected that such occurrences were likely much earlier when I walked over the course. The going was firm, as you would expect of cobbles, but slippery with spilled beer and wine, as you would expect of streets in which the populus had been having an outdoor party for more than a week.

There may have been the odd cat-call for the front-runners, but I honestly don't recall. And anyway, these *valientes* or bravehearts are sometimes the very ones who will hit out at a bull from behind the safety of a fence. This particular day's bull run had been a dangerous one, the locals said. One of Pamplona's most famous runners, Julen, a bald-headed veteran of some 20 years, was caught and gored in the head and stomach. This brought the result for the eight runs of this year's festival to Bulls 23, Humans 0.

When a local is wounded in the run, it becomes his brief moment of fame, the newspapers giving front-page coverage in full detail. Javier Diaz Faes had the best known backside in town when he was gored, resulting in a wound 40 centimetres long. Not content with interviewing the wounded, the press report the comments of the mother, wife, girlfriend and his chums down the pub who are very proud of him.

There is a big US presence at the event and the last runner to die was a young American. For this we can blame Ernest Hemingway,

TOLD YOU I WAS SICK

B. P. ROBERTS

MAY 17, 1929
JUNE 18, 1979

who made this festival of San Fermin internationally famous. For full details of the beauty, bravery etc, of it all, read his book *The Sun Also Rises*.

But my hero of this San Fermin was a Mexican, Enrique from Tijuana. He admitted he was not the bravest of runners and I saw him looking quite concerned or even terrified as he was cornered in a doorway by a bull which was eventually distracted from giving Enrique its full attention. It is Enrique's endurance which is outstanding. Having come all the way from Mexico he took part in all eight daily runs. You have to be up each day at 6 a.m. to be sure of getting a place for the 8 a.m. start. So the answer is to stay up all night and party. There is no respite after the race as the celebrations immediately begin all over again. Enrique told me he remembered having a short siesta on the Tuesday. Endurance is more important than speed in Pamplona.

ETA, NO

I AM in Spain doing a spot of moonlighting for *The Herald*'s arts department. It is a gruelling assignment involving watching two shows by Spanish companies who are appearing in this year's Edinburgh International Festival. I believe this comes under the general heading of dirty work, but someone has to do it.

It was a chance to get away from a gloomy Britain where Northern Ireland and its marching season dominated the news with the threat that the peace process would finally fail and terrorists on both sides might soon be back in full bloody employment.

It was not entirely cheery to arrive here and discover that Spain's own terror industry is still keeping itself busy. I arrived in San Sebastian to read that ETA had made an unsuccessful rocket attack on a local oil refinery. They had also opened what they call the 'summer campaign'. This consists of numerous bomb hoaxes and occasional small explosions on the beaches of Spain's Costas. They are usually careful to avoid killing any visitors while inflicting the maximum chaos on the Spanish tourist industry. It also ties up police resources with an extra two thousand drafted on to beach patrol this summer.

99

One day last week 15,000 holidaymakers had to be evacuated from the beaches at Lloret Del Mar. It was no big deal, unless you were a child on holiday and were banned from the beach.

The Spanish have become used to the nuisance that ETA's discredited campaign for Basque separatism now is. Usually it's just a matter of vandalism to road signs, telephone kiosks, and bank cashline machines. But this weekend ETA were back in the headlines with the kidnap of a politician who was a member of Spain's ruling party, the right-of-centre *Partido Popular*. But it was no political bigwig that they picked on. Miguel Angel Blanco was the PP councillor in the small town of Ermua between San Sebastian and Bilbao.

Miguel Angel was 29 years old and, from reading the details of his life, the only criticism that could be levelled at him was that he kept his lovely fiancée waiting with too long an engagement. Miguel Angel was kidnapped on Thursday and would be killed at 4 p.m. on Saturday if a number of ETA prisoners were not moved to a jail in the Basque country. It was a cowardly and ludicrous action by ETA. A bit like a Scottish terrorist group seizing wee Baillie Bill Aitken, a Glasgow Tory councillor, and using his life as a bargaining tool.

Spain was filled with revulsion and apprehension as the 48 hours ticked away. The people wore blue ribbons as a symbol of solidarity with Miguel Angel. They gathered in their city and town squares. Television channels displayed a

ED SERVES The HAGGIS at EDS WAREHOUSE RESTAURANT

ON RABBI BURNS BIRTHDAY!

blue ribbon permanently on the corner of the TV screen and cancelled normal programmes to cover the countdown to 4 p.m. Saturday.

ETA ignored this immense public protest and put two bullets in Miguel Angel's head. They couldn't even kill him properly. He was still alive when they dumped him outside San Sebastian. His family and fiancée had to undergo a further 11 hours of trauma before he was pronounced dead.

The Spanish people's revulsion and apprehension turned into rage and indignation. They were impotent against the invisible terrorists but not against Herri Batasuna, the political wing of ETA, which still attracts votes and returns MPs and councillors.

Crowds gathered outside HB headquarters chanting 'asesinos' and 'hijos de puta', the latter being Spanish for 'sons of bitches'. Some local HB offices were set on fire. But the most effective protest has been the well-ordered gatherings in every city square.

I stood on Sunday night in Bilbao's Plaza Mayou with 500,000 people and there was total silence. That message to HB and ETA was louder than any words. There has been a clamorous silence, too, from HB who have yet to comment far less condemn the killing of Miguel Angel. Attempts to talk to HB meet with no comment. I wanted to know what was so wrong with life in this part of northern Spain.

DROP YOUR PANTS & SKIRTS HERE!

EARLY BIRD $1.99

PLAIN ONLY!

The Basque country has its own devolved parliament and control over much of its own economy. And it is quite a vibrant economy with steelworks, shipyards, and car factories, the kind of things Scottish workers might remember.

The Basques also have other little things in life such as cheap and plentiful food and drink, not to mention Havana cigars at one-third of the price they are in Britain. Then there is the sunshine, but with enough rain to make their countryside as beautiful as the Scottish Highlands.

The Basques are not exactly suffering and most wish ETA and HB would stop fighting on their behalf. ETA have had their day. At one time they had a part to play when they stood up against the Franco dictatorship. They killed someone else called Blanco back in those days – Luis Correro Blanco, an admiral in Franco's navy and the man tipped to succeed him and keep the fascist regime going. On 20 December 1973, ETA blew him up in a spectacular explosion which sent the admiral's car up and over a Madrid tenement building. History has shown that by doing away with Franco's heir the ETA boys of 1973 did well.

Parents and grandparents in the crowd in Bilbao on Sunday night do not need reminding of the Franco days. Many of them would have been in a similar protest in 1975. On that occasion the demonstration was against Franco's police who had taken two ETA activists, still in their teens, out into the countryside and executed them.

At the weekend it was ETA who took a young Basque out into the countryside and executed him. ETA and HB are the new fascists of Spain.

IT'S A FUNNY OLD GAME

A VISIT to the World Cup in 1994 offered a view of the langauage of soccer as it might be when the Yanks finally colonise the sport:

A TV analyst on Team USA player Dooley: 'He is the centrepiece of the game plan . . . he will anchor the defence and handle the ball a lot . . .'

'He's been called over for an attitudinal reality check.' – American cable TV commentator on a Swiss player summoned to the touchline for a wee word from his coach.

'That was more efficient than American football. The 45 minutes took less than an hour to play.' – Sara Jordan, oil company executive to *The Herald* Diary at half-time during the Norway–Mexico game in Washington.

'If it's a draw at full-time, they play an extra 30 minutes. If it's still a draw, they take penalty kicks. If it's still a draw after that, the two team coaches go into the centre circle and have a fist-fight.' – *The Herald* Diary to Sara Jordan, who had enquired how tied games were decided in the knock-out section of the tournament.

'A square ball is a lateral pass. It does not refer to the shape of the ball.' – Dallas newspaper explaining the finer points of the game to its readers.

FOOTBALL is thriving in Scotland. Not the football that is controlled by Jim Farry and Co. of Park Gardens but the sort where chaps get together for a spot of fun. You remember fun – the element Farry and Co. have removed· from the game. The enjoyment is being had at soccer complexes all over Scotland. It is living proof that age does not wither nor beer-belly prevent grown men suffering from delusions of adequacy on a football pitch. You can tell the boys are enjoying themselves merely by reading the names of the teams in the various leagues: A Paisley team by the name of Plastic Thistle won their local league. Another title went to Dynamo Dreadful. A lower division was topped by Rab C. Milan.

Other notable names: Castlemilk Stanklifters – redolent of the good old days of street football. Charlton Pathetic, Partizan Below Grade, Pathetico Madrid, and Rank Rotten Rovers – all teams that seem to know their station in life.

Some Glasgow teams were AC Mature, One Foot in the Grave, Real Mince, Surreal Madrid Fish, Outer Milan, Unathletic Madrid, and Red Star Below Grade. Drink, featured, of course, with teams called Booze Brothers and Betty Ford Clinic.

A bunch of lads in Cumnock were so impressed by the quality of Dutch football, and Ajax in particular, that they called themselves Vims.

In a five-a-side tournament in Hamilton, competitors included Inter Marijuana, VD Milan, Simpledoria, the People's Front of Judea, Sexual Chocolate, Monklands Mafia, Hadjuk Spliff, Alcoholico Madrid, and Hashton Villa. The trophy was won by Mabozaritchie FC. The old lady who had to inscribe the trophy was told the team was named after the vice-president of Uganda who had a Scottish grandfather.

THE *Absolute Game* magazine, as part of a series on the Forgotten Ones, recalled the contribution over the years of Arthur Montford. Arthur, the passionate Scots fan with a microphone who urged our players to 'watch your back' and unashamedly celebrated every Scottish goal. Writer Alistair McSporran, eulogised Arthur as the 'genuine communicator'. By way of example he recalled an occasion when Scotland were playing Czechoslovakia. Scotland were behind with time ticking away. The ball went out of play on the nearside. Denis Law dashed over to take the throw-in. The ball-boy was not displaying the necessary urgency. The camera had zoomed right on to Law's face at the moment when he was clearly heard to shout: 'Hey, ya wee bastard, give us the effan ball.'

With some understatement, Arthur commented: 'There's Denis urging the ball-boy, quite correctly I may add, to get a move on with it.'

AC Milan is owned by TV magnate Silvio Berlusconi. Tottenham Hotspur has computer tycoon Alan Sugar. Rangers is in the financial fiefdom of David Murray's conglomerate. This connection between footie and big business spreads through the entire sport. We were hearing some details of the behind-the-scenes commerce at Glenafton, the Ayrshire junior team. Their cash appears to stem from dealing in the pigs' trotters future market. Club secretary John Tympany is a butcher who recently made quite a killing by purchasing 50,000 pairs of pigs' trotters when the price was low and selling when the market picked up. The New Cumnock club's finances appear to be in a healthier state than many of their senior rivals. They were recently able to outbid Ayr United for a player.

THE ITV *Chart Show* (we never missed it of a Saturday lunchtime) had a quiz question before and after commercial breaks. To coincide with a showing of the latest Simple Minds video, they asked: 'What team does Jim Kerr support?' And to make it easier for those who might not be aware of the crooner's footballing persuasion, they offered the choice of 'Glasgow Rangers or Celtic Rangers'. After the break we were informed that Mr Kerr supports Celtic Rangers. Wrong. His fave team is, of course, Celtic Rangers Thistle Clyde.

IN the *Celtic View* we find a listing for a St Fergus supporters club. Not an elevation to the sainthood for Fergus McCann, the saviour of Celtic, but a club which caters for fans from the towns of St Fergus and Forfar and surrounding areas.

A TEAM of researchers from Aberdeen University found it necessary to be in New York and Orlando during the World Cup in 1994 to study the behaviour of the Irish football fans. We offer some highlights from their report with our own more simplistic analysis:
* Ireland's fans' culture 'is largely an extension of the Irish carnivalesque'. (Irish football fans are a sociable bunch who like a wee drink and a song.)
* The Irish 'were not consistently involved in interaction with opposing fans. Apart from downtown Orlando, there were few public rituals of extended communication and exchange . . .' (Unfortunately, the Irish lads didn't get a chance to mingle with the girls from Brazil.)
* The Irish fans travelling to the USA had a very broad age, gender, and social class composition. (There's the oul fella off to New York, but he's having to

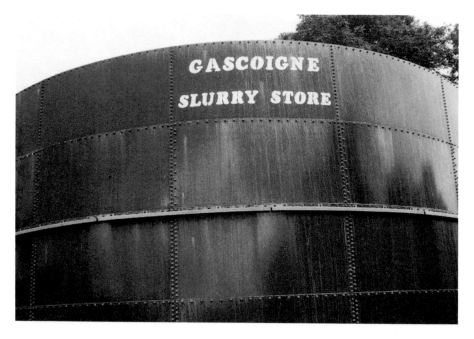

take herself because of the money she's skinned out of the house-keeping.)

* The World Cup underlined the game's function in allowing the Irish to express non-political sentiments of national and cultural identity. ('Jack's the Man! Ole! Ole! Ole!' Irish fan celebrates another fabulous draw, pausing only to buy a pint of stout for the queer fella sociologist from Aberdeen who keeps asking silly questions.)

THE Revd Bill Shackleton, Greenock pastor and humorist, told of one of his elders who does a commentary for a group of blind Morton supporters who sit beside him at home games. During one match, Morton were denied a penalty. One of the group leapt to his feet shouting in hot indignation the time-honoured advice for such occasions: 'Open your eyes, referee!'

ALSO heard at Cappielow: 'For goodness sake, Morton! Your defence is all higgledy-piggledy!'

AN Ayr United supporter who had travelled to Stranraer to see his team lose 2–1 consoled himself too deeply with draughts of ale. In the early hours of Sunday morning, he was discovered by police in a shop doorway. He told the cops he had booked into a bed and breakfast but could not find the establishment. Asked the name of the B&B, he replied that the keys bore the inscription

'Home and Garden'. This transpired to be the DIY store where the keys had been cut. The unfortunate fan's weekend had been further ruined by the fact that he had left his false teeth in a glass of water by his bedside in the B&B. Wherever it was.

MICHAEL Kelly, the former Celtic director, is nothing if not outspoken. In his book *Paradise Lost*, he did not miss and hit the wall when it came to delivering blunt and unflattering opinions on people and institutions:

* Of his erstwhile socialist colleagues on Glasgow District Council he said: 'The Labour Party in Glasgow despises ambition almost as much as it suspects talent.'

* He had a sideswipe at the Germans in a speech at a 'stupefyingly boring dinner' attended by both team officials when Celtic were playing away at Borussia Dortmund. He recalled: 'I finished by announcing the end of the function so that the Germans could get to the stadium and put towels on their seats.'

* Cousin Kevin, the Kelly of Michael's generation who got to be chairman of Celtic, is described variously as 'pathetic' and 'mumbling'.

* Another former Celtic chairman, Jack McGinn, was described as: 'The sort who struggles with past participles and who has difficulty with the pronunciation of "lunatic" . . .' 'McGinn,' he wrote, 'liked to allude to his background in newspapers, which may have given the impression that he was some kind of journalist. In fact he worked on the distribution side, calling on newsagents to check that they were getting the correct numbers of copies of the *Daily Express*. Such a skill, though a vital cog in any media empire, was not precisely the kind of experience that Celtic needed in the late 1980s.'

* Tom Grant's ability as stadium director was called into question. 'Grant was visited by a photocopier salesman, and on the basis of a promise of sponsorship he signed a deal which committed the club to over £120,000 on office equipment. Try as Chris (White, the Celtic company secretary) did to get us out of the deal, he found a legally binding contract had been signed by Grant before he ran to Chris with the problem . . . We had redundant photocopying machines falling out of every cupboard. The promised sponsorship never materialised.'

* Paul McStay was described as a player who 'is no captain' and who 'can't shoot for toffee'.

* The rebellious fans were put in their place geographically and sociologically with the reference to the final board meeting at Parkhead: 'I could hear the crowd

outside chanting "Michael Kelly's on the dole" before they made their way back to their peripheral houses.'

ONE of Celtic's best-selling videos during the club's lean years was said to be *Forty Great Celtic Throw-Ins*.

THERE were rumours that Rangers Pools supremo Hugh Adam, was a head-hunting target for the other cash-strapped half of the Old Firm. We can confirm that this was never on the cards despite some little local difficulties with Ibrox chairman David Murray. Mr Adam was heard to describe any move to Celtic Park as 'like tunnelling into the Alamo'.

A BUNCH of England fans found themselves in the middle of the Scots at a Hampden game. All very interesting, they thought, until they became aware of a Scottish fan urinating immediately behind them. One of the Englishmen turned round and said: 'I say! Have a care!'

To which the Tartan-tammied reply was: 'Whit's up, Jimmy? Ur yer boots lettin' in?'

DAVID Shaw of Glasgow told us the tale of a Maryhill man who emigrated to America in the 1960s. When he got off the boat in New York he saw a wee teepee with a cardboard sign saying 'Tonto The Memory Man – All Questions Answered. 25 cents'. He went in and asked: 'Hey Tonto, when did the Jags last win the Scottish Cup?'

Without hesitation Tonto replied, '1921. They beat Rangers 1–0.'

Twenty years later the Maryhill man had become a successful businessman and decided to fly home for a visit. On arriving at Kennedy Airport he saw a two-storey marble building in the shape of a teepee with a big neon sign 'Tonto The Memory Man – All Questions Answered. $10'. He decided to pay his respects. There was Tonto sitting on a golden throne. The man approached him and raised his hand. 'How!' he said.'A penalty in the 65th minute,' replied Tonto.

WHAT a life these sports reporters have. The Diary was especially impressed with the task handed to Roddy Forsyth – take sundry sporting Old Firm legends out to lunch and talk to them about their favourite football match of all time. Thus Roddy found himself in a one-to-one knife and fork situation with the legendary Slim Jim Baxter. But as Roddy said in the book, *Blue and True*: 'The restaurant was airy and cheerful and the menu was inviting. The problem was Baxter's choice of main course . . . liver. Considering that the man is a survivor of two liver transplants performed within a few days of each other, watching him put away a plateful of the stuff was distinctly weird'

The author's lack of appetite was noticed by the Greatest Transplanted Ranger who asked: 'Whit's up – are ye no' enjoying your food?'

STEPHEN O'Neill of Bearsden tells how his chum, whom we will call George from Torrance, had travelled to Marseille for a European Cup tie. George was still sporting a rather faded Rangers top, so old it bore the name C.R. Smith as sponsor. Out for a wee swally the night before the match, George was approached by a Marseille fan and asked to swap jerseys. He duly obliged, despite being told by a local that the French jersey was of such a vintage that it should have been in the Louvre and Marseille had a new sponsor and a different strip.

The next day George was on his way to the match when he was stopped by a Rangers fan with the request: 'Haw, Frenchy, dae ye want tae swap jerseys?' George noticed the Bear was wearing the latest Rangers away jersey. He pretended not to understand the request, but when the Rangers fan indicated by gesture the nature of the transaction, George said: 'Ah, oui!'

GOAT-ROPING

THE diary took a crash course in marketing-speak from douglas Hill, of Scottish Enterprise Tayside:

* We don't say we have several options. We say we have several balls in the air.
* We don't say we may be able to work together on this. We say we have synergistic qualities.
* We don't say, what use is this? We ask what are the concept benefits?
* We don't say I think we'll try and sell this outside Dundee. We say we're going global.
* We don't say we asked but they're not interested. We say they are unconverted inquiries.
* We don't stick two things together in an envelope. We nest.
* We don't have a percentage response. We have a pull. (For example, did you get a percentage response at the dancing last night?)
* We do not disagree. We non-concur.
* We do not have a meeting of the main decision makers. We have a goat-roping session. (To goat-rope is to tie something down and settle it once and for all.)
* We do not remove obstacles. We remove the rocks from the runway.
* We do not correct errors. We fine-tune, tweak, and generally nit-pick.
* We do not get better on the computers. We become more IT literate.
* We do not set objectives. We agree deliverables.
* We do not have a group of people exchanging ideas. We have cognate groups.
* We do not have changed priorities or even goalpost-moving. We have sea changes.
* We do not have folk doing things. We have people-driven initiatives.
* We do not have unemployed youngsters looking for jobs. We have skillseekers.
* We do not have situations where things are not working. We have

negative scenarios. When things are working we have positive scenarios.

* We do not get on with the job. We run with it.

* We do not agree. We all sing from the same hymn sheet.

* We do not allocate money. We ring-fence funds.

* We are not here to help. We facilitate.

* We do not say 'I'd better do this first'. We prioritise our in-trays.

* We do not hand out freebies. We make available company-specific promotional items.

* We do not take work home. We run it through our laptops.

* We do not tell folk what's going on. We cascade information.

* We do not pass on jobs we do not like. We empower staff.

* We do not just get on with things. We have a 'can-do' philosophy.

* We do not have important areas to concentrate on. We have strategic thrusts.

* We do not leave people on their own to answer all the phones. They are holding the fort.

* We do not have estimates of costs. We have ball-park figures.

* We do not have a load of leaflets. We have a family of brochures.

* We do not say 'That's not fair'. We say 'We're not competing on a level playing field'.

* We do not say 'What are you talking about?' We say 'I don't know where you're coming from'.

HOGMANAY

THE Diary examined the whole iconography of this great scottish ritual and placed it in the context of changing mores and cultural influences in the age of satellite broadcasting and the information superhighway. Or, as usual, we settled for funny stories, jokes and reminiscences.

DAVE Stormonth of Paisley has memories of a particularly hectic after-the-bells party. He was sitting, propped up against a wall. Various other figures were strewn about the room. 'Nobody stirred except the lone figure of my uncle who was tiptoeing between the bodies lifting up the occasional glass, sniffing it, and downing the contents. He soon realised I was watching him. He put his finger to his lips, bent down, and whispered in my ear: "This reminds me of the desert campaign, looking for watches."'

THE Diary's Hogmanay reminiscences kick off with a tale from Graeme Atha of East Comiston, Edinburgh, of a first-foot bearing gifts. The first-foot was indeed young and handsome. But also rather inebriated. The young man in search of some fresh air first asked if a window could be opened. This was done but it was not enough. In search of even greater quantities of crisp Ne'erday fresh air, the young man actually made his way into the garden.

But there was no improvement in his feeling of confusion and general unwellness. So much so that he was shortly to be observed leaning through the window into the dining room to be copiously sick. Certainly makes a change from a first-foot present of a lump of coal or a bit of shortbread.

THE story is set in the days after the Second World War when whisky was an expensive and scarce commodity. A chap is setting off on his first-footing rounds with the half-bottle snug in his hip pocket. The pavements are icy and he topples over. He feels a wetness in his nether regions and utters: 'Christ, I hope it's blood.'

A CUMBERNAULD man was taking an English friend on the Hogmanay rounds. The Englishman took kindly to the ritual, armed with a bottle of whisky, lumps of coal, and some of his mother's Christmas cake which had the icing scraped off in an attempt to make it to look like black bun. For the purpose of the tale, we have to mention that the English chap wore a wig, a handsome and expensive jet-black rug. One old lady, a bit of a traditionalist when it comes to Hogmanay susperstitions, was delighted to have this tall, dark chap as her first-foot.

As can happen, the first-foot celebrated rather too well and was eventually left in recovery mode on top of a bed. A little later, the lady's carnaptious Yorkshire terrier appeared chewing at what appeared to be the skin of a small animal. It was the first-foot's wig. Rather than express concern for her guest's loss of wig, the lady of the house demanded that he be removed from the house in case any more bad luck befell the household.

'And take that black bun with you as well,' she added, 'It's bliddy rotten.'

ERNEST Cook of Bishopton, Renfrewshire, offered a story which shows that the English will never really understand Hogmanay. When he was a young boy, his family moved south to Northampton. It was New Year's Eve, just before the bells, when it was noticed that the clock had stopped. Young Ernest offered to pop down the street and check the time on the town clock and return to 'let the New Year in'. While carrying out this mission, he was apprehended by a policeman who was not convinced by the lad's story about going out to check the time so he could be his family's first-foot. Ernest was duly deposited in the local nick and the family's first-foot was a tall, dark polis dispatched by the sergeant to fetch his father.

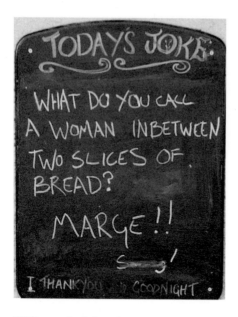

WE are indebted to the *Somerfield Magazine* for a pithy and unusual definition of Hogmanay. The publication is issued free to customers of Somerfield/Gateway supermarkets who know that:

'Hogmanay, the Scottish version of New Year, is the most celebrated event of the Christmas season and everyone has an "open-door" policy where passers-by can pop in for a New Year drink and a snack. Just before midnight everyone goes out the back door, walks around the house and enters through the front door to say goodbye to the old year and to welcome the new year.'

And the festivities go on according to the magazine: 'On 31 January people in Scotland have haggis because it is Robbie Burns Day named after a poem he wrote called *To A Haggis*.'

THE scene is Govan one New Year during the last war when it was a rare treat for a working man to have in his hands an entire bottle of whisky. Our man is making his way to first-foot some friends. In addition to the whisky, our man has also managed to purloin some oranges. He is making his way gingerly along the icy pavement when he slips and his precious cargo goes up in the air. Lying on his back, he reaches out for the whisky, manages to catch an orange as he hears the sound of a crashing bottle and sees the golden liquid spread tantalisingly across the pavement.

THE Hogmanay tradition appears to be alive and well in the royal burgh of Lanark where they still celebrate the Het Pint ceremony. Locals who turn up at the council offices at 9.45 a.m. on New Year's Day get a tot of mulled wine. Pensioners are given £1 coins. The practice dates back to the seventeenth century when the Earl of Hyndford left a bequest to provide a pint of hot spiced ale for 50 needy townspeople.

Nearby in Biggar they still have the Hogmanay bonfire. The tradition dates back unbroken almost 1000 years. During the war years when blackout regulations prohibited bonfires, the spirit of Hogmanay was kept going by lighting a candle under a bucket.

CUTTING REMARKS

A TOUCHING announcement in the acknowledgements section of the Lennox Herald newspaper. Among the list of thanks for help following their bereavement is one to a family friend 'for his uplifting spirit and cheerfulness, on his many visits his parting words, "Mind your heid on the lobby lamp" always left us laughing'.

FROM the personal columns of the *Ayrshire Post* :
'Lady Wanted – to waken gent evey day as near as possible 6.30 a.m. to 7.30 a.m. Early as possible to chap (knock) at window and ring bell often. State price (not too expensive if possible). Lady with phone. As near Whittlets direction as possible.'

THE following advert fairly brightened up the Work Wanted column of the *Dundee Courier*: 'Country-bred Swedish girl (17) searching for interesting positions on farm with livestock.'

Didn't they make a movie about that?

THERE is little of the spirit these days of Jackie Green, the legendary vendor of the *Evening Citizen* newspaper in Glasgow in the 1950s and 1960s. Jackie's rough and penetrating tones could be heard advertising stories that often were not in the newspaper. 'Terrible, horrible murder!' he would cry. Alternating with 'Terrible, horrible rape!'
    But Jackie was not without subtlety. 'Big city fraud! Twenty-three victims!' he would shout and, after selling another newspaper containing not a word about any fraud, would continue: 'Big city fraud! Twenty-four victims!'

THE Nuffield Hospital in Glasgow decided to advertise its infertility service in an Arabic magazine. A London advertising agency who specialise in such matters were asked to provide the

DAY OF THE WEEK	DATE	09:30 UNTIL 13:00	14:00 UNTIL 16:30
Monday	24-Jun-96	Open	Open
Tuesday	25-Jun-96	Possibly Open	Possibly Open
Wednesday	26-Jun-96	Possibly Open	Possibly Open
Thursday	27-Jun-96	Possibly Open	Possibly Open
Friday	28-Jun-96	Possibly Open	Possibly Open
Saturday	29-Jun-96	Possibly Open	Closed

OPENING HOURS FOR WEEK COMMENCING: 24-JUN-96

Arabic equivalent of the phrase: 'The joy of having a baby.' The Nuffield people duly received the artwork in Arabic at which they nodded sagely but uncomprehendingly and sent back, marked approved. Fortunately before the publication went to press, it was noticed that the Nuffield were inviting their Arab customers to come to Glasgow and savour the joys of a much earlier part of the process of making a baby.

A BEARSDEN reader with the splendid name H. Morton Macquaker wrote to point out a fine piece of estate-agent-speak.

Slater, Hogg and Howison, trying to flog a four-storey townhouse in Belmont Crescent in the West End of Glasgow, described the property as being situated in a 'desirable curved crescent'. Absolutely. All the best crescents are curved. Accept no straight substitutes.

WE were indebted to *Flicks*, a magazine free at a cinema near you, for the reason behind the change of title of the film of Alan Bennett's stage play *The Madness of George III* for foreign movie-goers. It was simply called *The Madness of King George*. It was feared Americans would ignore the film, having failed to catch parts one and two.

IN the 'new members' section of the *Journal of the Glasgow Chamber of Commerce* we found an entry for Maitlands Solicitors. The list of services they offer included 'commercial conveyancing, corporate work, travel and holiday law, trust and excretory work, civil literature . . .' The bit about literature was puzzling, but what really concerns us is this 'excretory work'. Should it be executry work? Or will Maitlands really handle anything?

EVERY silver cloud has a dark lining, as the saying nearly has it. What are we talking about, we hear you ask. Actually it's the front-page headline from the *Buteman* newspaper published in sunny Rothesay: 'Peace in Ireland a threat to Scottish tourism.'

GOOD to see that *Scotland on Sunday* carried an article in Urdu by Bashir Maan, a leading Asian–Scot. Not having the Urdu, we didn't understand a word. But we are sure it was very interesting. Unlike a local paper we know of who recruited an Asian shopkeeper to contribute a column in Urdu. The item had been running for a month before the Urdu-less editor was informed that his columnist was using the space to promote the latest bargains available at his cash and carry.

STRATHCLYDE University's alumni magazine, *Interface*, featured a list of the boys and girls who have went on and done good. Amid the various captains and captainesses of industry and commerce we find this entry: 'Mingay, David (BA Psychology, 1981) is now "out" after serving five years for fraud. He would love to hear from any of the old gang, except of course those b******* who grassed on him and others to whom he still owes money!'

AN advert appeared in the window of a shop in Kilwinning with, we are assured, the following wording: 'For sale. Genuine leopard-skin coat. Spotless condition.'

A SMALL ad in a local paper, under the heading 'Clocks and watches for sale'. It reads: 'Cuckoo clock. Very annoying cuckoo clock for sale. Someone hurry and buy it, before the cuckoo gets it.'

THOSE who pen sporting headlines in the tabloid reaches of the media normally have to corrupt footballers' names in the search for pithy phrases, *viz* Gazza for Gascoigne. No such problems with Middlesbrough striker Uwe Fuchs who was red-carded in a home match against Sheffield United, leading to the heading: 'Fuchs Off at Boro!'

FROM the personal columns of the *Stirling Observer*, a recent unparalleled career opportunity for OAPs: 'Cleaning lady of the older fashioned type to scrub and polish linoleum, black lead grate, clean brass, and normal household duties for widower. In old cottage up a cart-track road one mile from Gartmore village. One day per fortnight. Must have transport, horse, bike or car.'

THE *Scots Magazine*, that doucest of journals, carried a letter from an Australian reader. It was headed 'What a Difference!' and told of the down-under-person's experience while on holiday in the Highlands. The writer, a Mr Ian McCrae, JP, of Sydney, had some harsh words to say about 'white settlers' running hotels and B&B establishments who offer a cold welcome and high prices. But Mr McCrae singled out one Scottish-owned B&B for particular praise.

'Just to prove that Scotland is a home away from home for the weary traveller, we found a bed and breakfast near Kyle of Lochalsh, run by a Mr and Mrs Macmillan at Grianan House,' he wrote. We didn't want to leave. After all, this is what we came all the way from Australia to find. We will be back next year. Thank you,

Donald and Zena, also young Donald, for restoring our faith in Scotland and the Scots.'
• Donald Macmillan (32), son of the owners of Grianan House, was soon after found guilty at Dingwall Sheriff Court of murdering Helen Torbet and concealing her body at the guest house.

COMMUNITY *Outlook*, the magazine for district nurses and health visitors, had a feature, 'Suppositories: a pull-out-and-keep guide.'

THE *Oban Times*, bulwark of the west Highland establishment astonished readers with the following engagement anouncement: 'Small-Ritchie. Both fam-

approximately 300 members, like missionaries of the open road they preach the gospel of Jesus Christ and try to break down the barriers between bikers and the general public.'

THE *Largs and Millport News* carried a letter from a man seeking assistance from the good people of this douce seaside area. He used to live in Largs but had moved. He wrote: 'I am a widower as my wife died in 1988. I am very keen on finding out the whereabouts of the metallic suitcase full of *Playboy* magazines which I left in the garage of the Greenock Road address. We thought the magazines had been lost in the removal. I was a collector.' He added: 'We have many wonderful, happy memories of Largs . . .'

ilies are devastated to announce the engagement between M'Titza Small and M'Bosa Ritchie, both of 6 Woodlea, Barbreck, by Lochgilphead.'

GREAT Corrections of Our Time. *GQ* magazine had to eat humble pie with the following retraction: 'Alongside the article *Outlaw Bikers* in the June 1993 issue of *GQ* we ran photographs which we said showed members of the Hells Angels. Unfortunately one of the photographs was of Alan Lowther, who is president of the Christian Motorcyclists Association. The Christian Motorcyclists Association is composed of an interdenominational spectrum of bike riders and enthusiasts (including clergymen) all united by their love of Christ. Formed in 1979 and numbering

IN a publication called the *British Humanities Index* we found the following description of a text by one Melissa Raphael on religious experience and feminism: 'Brings together constructivist epistemology and feminist study of religion to provide phenomenological evidence that numinous consciousness is not the immediate, *sui generis* essence of religious experience that Rudolf Otto believed it to be. Contemporary gynocentric spiritualities in which women celebrate their psychobiological difference as itself is a necessary medium of religious experience, have no interest in protecting the holy from the limitations of its immanence.'

IT is a doleful but necessary task in a newspaper to acknowledge and apologise for mistakes. The *Inverness Courier* had to don the sackcloth when it made a mistake in the details of the appointment of a new clerk to Inverness presbytery of the Church of Scotland. At the end of the correction was added the biblical reference 'Psalm 51, verse 3' which, as keen students of the good book will know, reads: 'I acknowledge my transgressions and my sin is before me.'

ATTRIBUTED to the *Cape Times* in South Africa is a story of unexplained deaths in the Pelonomi Hospital in the Free State region.

'For several months, our nurses have been baffled to find a dead patient in the same bed every Friday morning,' a spokesperson told reporters.

There was no apparent cause for any of the deaths and exhaustive checks of equipment, including air-conditioning for bacteria, produced no solution to the mystery. An answer was eventually found. It seems that every Friday morning a cleaner would enter the ward, remove the plug that powered the patient's life-support system, plug her floor polisher into the socket and go about her work. When she had finished she would put the other plug back in and leave, unaware that the patient was dead.

'She could not, after all, hear the screams and eventual death rattle over the whirring of the polisher.'

The cleaner was warned as to her future conduct and the Free State health and welfare department arranged for an extra socket to be put in.

HEADLINE: 'Shamed bishop seeks missionary position'.

A GRAPHIC court report from *The Buteman*. Under the heading 'Eyes and ears lost in Pavilion brawl', we read: 'A witness instructed by Sheriff Herald to parade before the jury to display his mutilated ear, watched with his one eye by the accused, who had lost his other in the same incident, were testament to a violent brawl at a Pavilion disco in September.'

WITH THE LIBERAL DEMOCRATS

IF the Liberal Democrats are not careful they will get a reputation for being interesting. At their Brighton conference they have given the go-ahead to get stoned without the attentions of the Bill. But the reality is somewhat different. Immediately after the vote to legalise cannabis, the Diary conducted a straw poll of Lib Dem delegates in the foyer of the Grand Hotel, the conference meeting place where policy is formed, where the movers move and the shakers shake.

It was a simple question: 'Hey man, do you know where I can score some dope?'

Lord Jenkins of Hillhead displayed an insouciance unbecoming of a former MP for the West End of Glasgow by replying: 'I'm sorry, I don't know what you're talking about.'

Emma, a young Lib Dem from Leeds, replied: 'You'll have to ask some older Liberals. They're the ones who voted for it. They're easy to spot. They'll be wearing sandals and beads.'

A lady called Marietta Crichton-Stuart, who denied being one of the Bute Crichton-Stuarts and had a badge saying she was from Vauxhall in south London, said we should try Brixton if we wanted the said illegal substances.

We had to cut short our straw poll when we asked Trevor, a Lib Dem conference steward, if he knew where we could get a hold of some cannabis. He said he didn't but he had a policeman friend who might be interested in our request. We fear that Trevor is not quite in the liberal wing of the Liberal movement.

A CONFERENCE fringe meeting appeared to be a positive approach to law and order. It was titled 'Let's Kill All the Lawyers'. The snag was that it had been organised by the Law Society, the solicitors' trade union, and was in

fact a *cri de coeur* for us all to be far nicer to lawyers and presumably give them even more money. The message to kill lawyers was sympathetically received by at least one person in the function room of the Old Ship Hotel, Brighton. Step forward Maria, the waitress who was serving the wine. As a qualified lawyer without a job she would fully endorse both concepts that we should kill off some older people in the profession or accommodate some new starts.

WE confess to turning up at the fringe meeting 'Press for Change – Seeking Status and Rights for all Transexual People' expecting to find loads of chaps in frocks. The fringe meeting on transexualism turned out to be one of the more informative sessions of the day. Dr Ellis Snitcher explained that the whole situation is caused when there are crossed wires between the foetus's genitalia which are formed at five weeks in pregnancy and the sexual part of the brain, the hypothalymus, which comes onstream at seven months.

Transexualism is thus perfectly natural and the Lib Dems are fighting for a parliamentary Bill which will give them a fair deal. At the moment, a male-to-female transexual who falls foul of the law will end up in a men's prison. Not a great vote-winner, you might have thought, this giving succour to transexuals. But, it transpires, the meeting chairperson Mark Rees used to be called Brenda. He won his local government seat in Tunbridge Wells recently despite, or perhaps even because of, a *News of the World* report saying that the wispy bearded Lib Dem candidate was the darling of the disaffected Tories.

The closest we came to observing cross-dressing at the Lib Dem conference was a lady in full kilt, Harris tweed jacket, yellow T-shirt and tartan socks. And a sporran. Ladies don't wear sporrans, we said to her.

'I know,' said Shirley, an English enthusiast of Scottish country dancing from Essex. 'It's my shoulder bag which I find more comfortable to wear round my waist.'

And before you ask, no, we don't know what's worn under an Essex girl's kilt.

OUR appetite had been more than whetted for the social side of the Liberal Democrat conference when we read party leader Paddy Ashdown's message to the troops: 'Don't forget to leave your window slightly ajar, just in case.'

This was not, however, an injunction from Paddy, who has a certain reputation in shagging matters, for delegates to have a bit of fun. He was merely recalling his experiences at a previous conference when he returned to his B&B extremely late and had to shin up the drainpipe to get to his bed for an hour of sleep before the next day's session.

The reality of conference nocturnal activity is more mundane. It is 10 p.m. and in the hotel lounge there is a meeting on housing problems in peripheral areas.

CONFESSIONS OF A CYNIC IN AT THE DEEP END

LOURDES, JULY 1996

DAY 1: While many Glasgow Fair traditions vanish, one persists – that of the pilgrimage by the Roman Catholic faithful to the shrine at Lourdes. As the Glasgow pilgrims arrived on Fair Friday in this small Pyrennean town, their Edinburgh counterparts were leaving. The Glasgow contingent will in turn be replaced by Lanarkshire Tims as the pattern of pilgrimage closely follows the old Trades holiday.

I must confess that it was neither tradition nor piety which brought me to Lourdes, but opportunism in hitching a cheap lift on a pilgrim's plane on the way to take in some of the action in the Tour de France cycle race. The great bicycling circus passes through Lourdes on its way to Pamplona in northern Spain.

I had been told to expect much rattling of rosary beads as the plane took off from Glasgow Airport. Lady pilgrims are especially partial to saying a few 'Hail Marys' and 'Glory Be to the Fathers' to ease the tension of the flight. This can be much to the consternation of the chartered airline trolley girls intent on flogging their duty free goods.

In the event it was a chorus or two of 'Ave, Ave, Ave Maria' which saw us off. It is as well to have someone up there on your side just in case. (For the benefit

of readers unfamiliar with the above hymn, Ave, Ave is Latin for Hail, Hail.) And for readers unfamiliar with the story of Lourdes and who may not have seen the movie starring Jennifer Jones, here is a brief history. The Catholic Church believes that the Virgin Mary made 18 apparitions here in 1858 to Bernadette Soubirous, a 14-year-old peasant girl.

Fuelled by seven miraculous cures in that year alone, and directed by an astute local clergy, Lourdes was on its way to religious fame and commercial fortune. Today with five million visitors a year it is the world's brand-leader shrine. I admit to a deeply ingrained cynicism which makes it difficult to see Lourdes as anything other than a religous theme park. Around the tiny caves by the River Gave, where the apparitions are said to have occurred, has arisen a massive infrastructure.

The Lourdes churches reach to the skies and also dig to the depths. On the grotto site there is a complex of basilicas, crypts, and chapels with lofty spires grander than most cathedrals. More recently there has been built an underground space, the Basilica of St Pius X, which can hold services for 30,000 when it's the case of indoors if wet.

Of course, Marian Merchandising is to the fore. Jesus may have chased the money-lenders and the merchants from the temple, but they are here in Lourdes in abundance. Images of the Virgin Mary are available in many sizes and shapes, from a plastic holy water container at a few francs to a five-foot statue complete with neon halo at £400.

There is, or course, tackiness. A penholder in the shape of a grand piano with Mary on the lid. Plastic grottoes, fully lit up and with running holy water. I couldn't find the legendary cuckoo clocks from which the Virgin pops out on the hour and half-hour. So the award for the most tasteless object must go to the plastic photograph of the bloodstained face of Christ on the Cross. The photo changes when seen from different angles. At first the eyes are closed, then they open. Whatever the intention was for the artefact, the result is that Jesus, in the midst of his agony, is winking at passers-by.

The Lourdes guidebook justifies the souvenir shops as 'necessary as people do not wish to forget the graces of God received and make them known to others'.

Of the 410 hotels in Lourdes, the Stella Matutina is not the grandest, but is perhaps the friendliest – which is why it is the favourite of Scottish pilgrims. Jeanette, the lady in charge, possibly acting upon information from Margaret, the Universal

Travel courier, that I am a FP (Failed Pape), has put me in the room which was always used by the late Cardinal Gray. There is a photo of the cardinal on one wall. On another there is a photo of Cardinal Gray and the Pope and Cardinal Gray's wee dug, Rusty. There is also a giant crucifix and below it a prie-dieu upon which Cardinal Gray knelt to pray.

I related my good fortune to Cardinal Thomas J. Winning, who is with the Glasgow pilgrimage, and he said he wondered who had got the prie-dieu. But being a very down-to-earth Prince of the Church, he was happy to settle for the room with the fridge. Despite his busy schedule, Cardinal Winning always finds time for the Lourdes pilgrimage. This year he is probably the highest ranking churchman present, but he goes around in his quiet Wishaw way in the simple garb of an ordinary priest. Not for him the pomp and ceremony and trappings – unlike some higher-ups of other countries we could mention, but won't (okay, it's the Italians).

Meanwhile, a quiet attempt at a conversion process appears to be going on here. Jeanette, la patronne, has furnished me with a book on the miracles of Lourdes. The blessed Margaret of Universal has given me the Glasgow Pilgrimage Medal, complete with tartan ribbon, and has promised a full tour of the Lourdes experience.

Slightly more worrying is that there is a group of young Glasgow people in town and one of the leaders, John, aka Pele because he is rotten at football, has proposed a wee pub crawl. It is to be followed the next day by a penitential Mass and then a look at how the young people (and not a few older Scots) spend their holiday helping their sick pilgrim compatriots. John, aka Pele, is also suggesting a bath in the healing water of Lourdes. Will it work?

DAY 2: Lourdes manages to be bustling yet peaceful at the same time. With five million visitors a year, its shops, hotels, and cafés are busy and the streets teem with people who look as if they are on holiday. But there is an absence of unnecessary noise and a distinct calm amid the throng. For Lourdes is all about bringing relief, or hope, or release to the 300,000 ill and infirm who visit the shrine each year. Most of the other visitors are here to help the sick.

With so much illness and human suffering to meet the eye, Lourdes should be a depressing place. Instead, it is quite uplifting. John and Eamon are two of the Glasgow squad in Lourdes this week to act as *brancardiers*. This French word means 'stretcher bearer', but their duties can be anything from fetching a cup of tea to pushing a wheelchair.

The two have been coming to Lourdes, during their holidays and at their own expense, for more than 15 years. John says he gets more back from the experience than he could ever give. Like the time a young man dying of cancer took him out for a pint to cheer him up. Eamon says that even after all these years he is not sure if he knows what to make of Lourdes, but he keeps coming back.

Down in the hot and steamy basement laundry of the Accueil Notre Dame, the hospital which houses the sick, a retired Glasgow teacher is spending her Fair holiday washing and ironing soiled clothing and sheets. Others are scrubbing the floors of this aged institution. It is difficult to believe in apparitions of the Virgin Mary and in miraculous cures such as the 65 claimed for this French grotto, but there is no doubt about the many small miracles of human kindness which occur daily.

A visit to Lourdes is described in the guidebook as 'a plunge into spirituality to find oneself'. The Glasgow *brancardiers* have prescribed for this cynic a physical and bracing plunge into the bath at the Lourdes grotto. There are 17 baths cut into the rock and they are filled with the water from the very spring uncovered by St Bernadette nearly 150 years ago. The baths are mainly for the very ill but able-bodied pilgrims can

also go through the process. I am sure the Glasgow boys' main concern was for my physical and spiritual wellbeing and the fact that the water is freezing (or 'fresh' as the guidebook describes it) had nothing to do with it.

The book also says that to take a bath is 'only an exterior sign of what God asks of us. Thus a confession well made is preferable to a bath'. I must confess that I was put off both by the low temperature and the fact that the water is changed only twice a day.

The Lourdes holy water is prized for its healing powers. The spring produces 122,000 litres each day, which is just as well considering the prodigious quantities carted away in containers by pilgrims.

St Bernadette herself said: 'It is

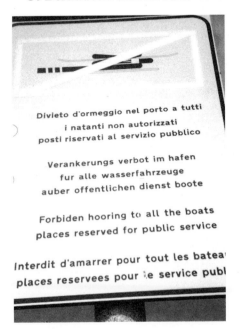

Divieto d'ormeggio nel porto a tutti
i natanti non autorizzati
posti riservati al servizio pubblico

Verankerungs verbot im hafen
fur alle wasserfahrzeuge
auber offentlichen dienst boote

Forbiden hooring to all the boats
places reserved for public service

Interdit d'amarrer pour tout les batea
places reservees pour le service publ

not the quantity that counts.' This is also the philosophy of a well-known Glasgow chap (no names) who promised quantities of Lourdes water to friends back home but did the sensible thing of taking only a little and diluting it with Loch Katrine's finest.

I saw an Edinburgh man showing an equally fine example of conservation when he set off for the grotto on the last day of his trip with a recently emptied whisky half-bottle as his container.

This seems an appropriate juncture to mention the Irish impact on Lourdes. The presence of many visitors from the Emerald Isle is to be expected. But a plethora (or should that be a begorra?) of Irish bars? A Tara Hotel? O'Flynn's Tea Shop? They're all there. Not to mention the St Laurence O'Toole Little Flower religious souvenir shop, complete with shamrocks on the sign.

I imagine that this St Laurence O'Toole might have been a bit of Irish mischief, perhaps based on that actor in the film *Lawrence of Arabia*. But no he was a Dublin martyr, said a lady in the Irish bar at the Hotel Astoria. This is the very bar, by the way, where the Nolan Mother, who gave the world the Nolan Sisters, once entertained the guests.

Yes, there is laughter in Lourdes. Much of it from or occasioned by the young people. Cardinal Thomas J. Winning recalls sharing a lunch table with some Glasgow youngsters, not yet teenagers and very unused to the French food being served. A seafood dish, served in the shells from which the clams had come, was particularly confusing for one boy. Observing the Cardinal tucking in he asked: 'Why are you eating out of the ashtray?'

When I said earlier that Lourdes was a quiet place I was not including the Italians. It is in their nature to be voluble, even when queuing up to visit the grotto itself. Every 15 minutes or so the Tannoy system issues a loud 'Sssh' which can only be meant for our Italian cousins.

The only other loud noise encountered at Lourdes is at a charismatic service in the huge underground basilica, where the rhythmic music and hand-clapping would not disturb the quiet Lourdes air. It was all a bit frenzied as priests and nuns swayed or whirled around with the faithful in great circles to the upbeat sound of hypnotic music. All this is meant to stir the emotions and break down barriers, but it looked to this veteran of the staid church of the 1950s like hocus-pocus meets the hokey-cokey. Dancing with nuns was never on the agenda.

The processions around the shrine are more formal and offer a much more moving spectacle. Except that they are not for spectators. I was standing watching when I was berated by a dapper elderly French gentleman of military bearing with the leather braces symbol of the *brancardier*. I didn't follow all of what he said but the gist of it was that I shouldn't be standing there when I could be helping push a wheelchair.

Lourdes can be a lonely place for those of little faith.

BETTE DAVIS PIES . . .

WE have been inundated by a veritable flood, indeed a banquet, of entries for the food song competition instigated by Restaurant Splash, the city's newest and one of its highest nosheries. We pass on some of the choice cuts to date:

Jim Gracie of East Kilbride suggests that if you like classical music with your food, you could try Vivaldi's Four Seasonings and that if you like a drink with your meal you might fancy Beethoven's Moonlight Sanatogen.

Whale Meat Again has been suggested by numerous correspondents, including Jim, who also suggests combining Indian food with classical music, thereby arriving at The William Tell Overture (popadom, popadom dom dom).

Hugh Fulton of Kilmarnock suggests a main course of Moon Liver or Aioli Have Eyes for You and proposes as dessert Sweet Georgia Brown. We have also had

Semolina in my Mind, Peggy Suet (not a dish we'd fancy on its own), Don't be Gruel and Bette Davis Pies.

FROM the tons of puns we bring you that ditty about the slightly surreal sailing craft, The Pie Boat Song, and the even stranger line from George Thomson of Lanark, 'Somewhere over the Rainbow, way a Pie'.

Alyson Raworth suggests Mousses Robinson, The Impos-

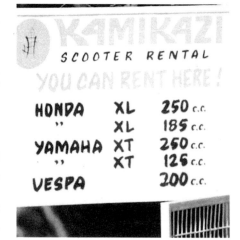

130

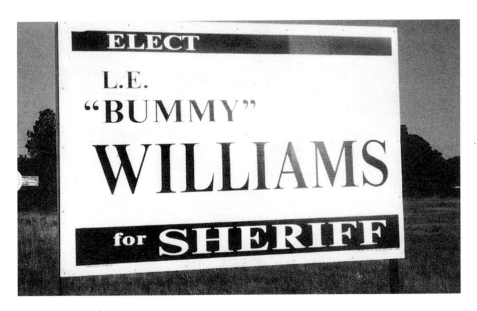

sible Bream, and, claiming that it is edible, Snot Unusual.

Stuart Bett of Balloch sent us several Scottish suggestions, including The Bannocks of Bonnie Dundee, which he says should be made with The Flour of Scotland, and also shares with us the information that just off the flower market in Amsterdam there is an Indonesian restaurant called Suki Bumi.

Vance Carson of Govan is in the running with something that the Diary would truly like to try, An Itsy Bitsy Teeny Weeny Yellow Polka Dot Linguini and that old Elvis number about poverty, deprivation and thick cream, In the Gâteau, and so is David Walker of Kilmacolm with a huge contribution, including that Neil Sedaka song about the woman full of holes, Colander Girl, and that

plea from wimp eaters, Save All your Quiches for Me.

ALSO from the song-menu mailbag:

Instant Korma

If I Only Had Thyme

Mayonnaise Have Seen the Glory

Put your Sweetbreads a Litttle Closer to the Phone

Chowmeiny Roads Must a Man Walk Down

Oh What a Beautiful Mornay

I'm Dreaming of a White Pudding

Wake Up Little Sushi by Buddy Holly

Tears on my Pilau

Green Grow the Rashers O'

I Remember Choux

Another One Bites the Crust

Wake Up Little Stovie

These Goulash Things

The Battered Bridie by Smetana

I Spam What I Spam

The Bridie Song
The Frying Game
It Doesn't Batter Anymore
Hey Mr Margarine Man
Skip to the Loo, my Darling (the curried version)
Anything by Smokie Robinson and the Mackerels
Careless Wispa
Everything I Chew, I Chew It for You
Send Me the Pilau That You Dream On
I Had a Girl, Doner Was Her Name
I Got Plenty of Mutton
Save All your Cous-Cous for Me

My Whey
Special K Sera, Sera
The Sheep, Sheep Song (It's in his Haggis)
Gnocchi Three Times on the Ceiling If You Want Me
There's a Prawn Shop on the Corner
Some Day I'm Gonna Write the Stovie of my Life
Focaccia a Falling Star
It Ain't Messy Celery Soup
As Time Goes By (What do you mean this has nothing to do with food? Altogether now: 'You Must Remember This, Haggis Is Just Haggis')
The Ballad of Davy Croquette
Rainy Days and Sundaes Always Get Me Down
Swing Low, Sweet Haricot
Rennies from Heaven
The Wurst of Sydney Devine
It's a Long Way to Piccalilli
Don't Fry for Me, I'm a Vegan
These Are a Stew of my Favourite Things
Stop your Pickling, Jock,
A Ricicle Made for Two
Don't Put your Daughter on the Stodge Mrs Worthington
Stand by your Flan

NO FOOTBALL, PLENTY OF COLOUR

ON your behalf we are in Monaco for a spot of world cup football with the Tartan Army. Except that these days the lads are so polite and ambassadorial they are more like the Tartan Corps Diplomatics (TCD).

6.30 a.m., Glasgow Airport: Some things never change. The chap in the kilt has set off the bleeper at security check-in with his tin of Irn Bru. In the bar at international departures the tartan-clad fans are four-deep at the bar. They have obviously not read Jim Farry's advice in the Guidance Notes for members of the SFA Travel Club – 'Do not turn up at the stadium drunk.'

Jim Farry gets quite evangelical on the subject of the fans' behaviour. 'Standards in our lives are subject to pressures. Let us maintain together the high standards displayed by Scotland's supporters and enhance the image of Scotland.'

7.10 a.m.: The bar appears to have run out of all draught beers, leaving the Bears free to go and buy their duty free. We are beginning to worry about Mr Farry's guidance notes.

7.30 a.m.: The girl at gate 27 announces to the lounge-full of fans wearing sundry soccer outfits, 'Monarch Airlines reminds passengers that no football colours are permitted on this flight.' It is early enough for some to believe her for a moment. One passenger is wearing full dinner jacket and bow tie. He has heard you need such kit to get into the Monte Carlo casino where he plans to spend some time and wager some money.

8.30 a.m.: The captain has reminded us of the airline rules about not smoking on the plane, or drinking your duty free. This has served to encourage the Bears in front to smoke and quaff their own whisky and vodka. Luckily the captain did not bother to remind passengers to refrain from sexually harassing the cabin crew.

9 a.m.: Our first language problem of the trip. The largest of the Bears has asked one of the Gatwick-based air crew for 'another cutla thay wee rolls'. It finally gets through that what is required is 'mair breid'. There are a few English accents among the TCD,

including a Sheffield man who has hardly missed a Scotland trip in 25 years. Unlike members of the Scotland football squad, he doesn't even qualify because his grandfather was Scottish. He just doesn't like England when it comes to following football. When there isn't a Scotland international, he follows Wales.

11.30 a.m., French time: Here we are on the tarmac at Nice airport, waiting for our bus to whiz us direct from plane to hotel. The Bears feel it is now safe to smoke despite those aviation fuel tankers parked 20ft away.

12.30 p.m.: Eddie the courier from Passport Travel informs us that it is Mardi Gras in Nice, an event similar in style if not in scale to the Carnival in Rio de Janeiro. The town will be wild tonight, he says, with much opportunity *pour chercher les femmes* or even have a beer. Eddie adds that, judging by the look of us lot, the second option is more likely. A dissenting voice in an north-east of Scotland accent says he has heard that there is 'a lot of rich old tottie on the Riviera'. Dream on, the Brechin Gigolo.

1 p.m.: Lobby of Hotel Climat. This gigolo thing is going too far; a kiltie is showing his bare backside to a party of French ladies of a certain age who are enjoying it far too much.

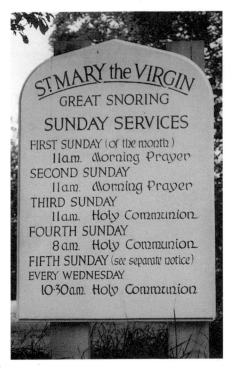

ST MARY the VIRGIN
GREAT SNORING

SUNDAY SERVICES

FIRST SUNDAY (of the month)
   11a.m. Morning Prayer
SECOND SUNDAY
   11a.m. Morning Prayer
THIRD SUNDAY
   11a.m. Holy Communion
FOURTH SUNDAY
   8a.m. Holy Communion
FIFTH SUNDAY (see separate notice)
EVERY WEDNESDAY
   10·30a.m. Holy Communion

1.30 p.m.: The bus is still waiting to leave for the game in Monaco. The trouble is not just that the lads are having a last drink, some of them are still putting on their make-up. With a children's face-painting kit purchased from a nearby toy shop, saltires and lions rampant are busily being applied.

2 p.m.: As we arrive in Monaco, Eddie from Passport announces that we are all welcome to join him on his yacht for a drink after the game. It's the big white one on the left-hand side of the harbour. And then it's on to John Collins's house for a party.

3 p.m.: It transpires you can get into the casino wearing trainers, jeans, and a Scotland top. The casino is a gloriously marbled and gilded building, a bit like Glasgow City Chambers with slot machines and gaming rooms. (Memo to Glasgow City Council: We may have an idea here for reducing the city's budget deficit.)

3.30 p.m.: In the square outside the casino, currency is disappearing almost as quickly in the bars as it did at the roulette table. It's £5 a beer, but the entertainment is beyond price. It is a contest between Japanese tourists and passing delegates to the 37th Monaco International TV Festival as to who are the most bemused by the garb and deportment of the TCD. The Japanese girls win when they ask for volunteers to pose with the fans for a photo and are rewarded by a Scot sticking his head up his pal's kilt to make an unusual souvenir snap.

5.30 p.m.: On the promenade a piper is leading elements of the TCD with that well-known pibroch Doh, a Deer, a Female Deer. Nearby, the Sheffield Scottish supporter is leading a song about 'sad English bastards'.

6.30 p.m.: On the way to the stadium, Stade Louis II, for the game, a party of young Monagasques in fancy dress are on

their way to an evening out at the carnival. They meet one of our number who is wearing trousers, jacket, waistcoat, tie, scarf, and socks, all in different tartans. 'Are you a clown, or are you Scottish?' they ask. As we write this, Scotland have not yet beaten Estonia and it's far too close to call.

Footnote: The result was Estonia 0, Scotland 0.

THE NAME GAME

GLASGOW university has a psychology lecturer called Dr Dick Dafters who is an expert on Ecstasy.

CHIEF executive of the Hykee Lock, which specialises in security systems for cars, is one Don Crooks.

SPOKESPERSON for the Army in Scotland is one Nigel Sargeant.

MANAGING director of Related Fluids Ltd of Cupar is a Mr Jonathan Spittle. The finance director of Manchester United is a Mr Launders. A fire-place shop in Edinburgh is called Hearth of Midlothian.

STONELAW parish church, Rutherglen, has a church officer called Mr Burke who works closely with the organist, Mr Hare.

PEOPLE say the nicest things about the Diary. Such as: 'I had a delivery of manure last week and I immediately thought of you. Nothing personal. It's just that the contractor who delivered the dung was a Mr Smellie.'

A MR Bounce of Brighton ran a bouncy castle business which lived up to its name by going into receivership.

SCOTTISH Discount of Glasgow offers a full range of financial services to businesses. Ask for a Mr Derek Money.

THE man who owns the ice-cream shop in Millport is a Mr Cool.

IAN Drain works for Deveron Water Systems in East Kilbride.

A COURSE tutor with Health and Safety (UK) Ltd is one Rex Careless.

137

CO-2
EGREMONT·FIRE DEPT.
WE SERVE WITH PRIDE
STEAK DINNER
SUNDAY OCT. 16

BIRMINGHAM Heartlands Hospital has an anaesthetist by the name of Dr Judith Gasser.

THE Scotland B cricket team's line-up for the match against Durham University includes one Graham Hurlbatt.

THE charge-hand responsible for planting trees in the Castlemilk area with the company Landwise is a certain George Twigg.

A COMPANY called Telephone Techniques from Leamington Spa, Warwickshire, offers courses on Handling Incoming Calls and Customer Care. The lady in charge is one Beryl Blower.

THE customer relations manager of Qantas airlines is Trevor Bluff.

THE Fairfield Road Surgery in Inverness has a Dr William Ross and a practice nurse Di Cromarty.

ON a recent list of potential jurors at Kilmarnock Sheriff Court was to be found one Norman Bates, occupation slaughterman.

THE *Westmoreland Gazette* of Cumbria runs a Spot the Dog competition based on snaps from sheepdog trials. One of the outlets where readers may leave their entries is a newsagent called D&H Woof.

GLASGOW University veterinary hospital had a post-graduate student called Hilde de Rooster.

A HIGH heid yin in the Norwich Union's healthcare division is a lady called Heidi Banger.

CHAIRMAN of North West Water is one Sir Desmond Pitcher.

FROM the Scottish Law Directory we see that Charles Wood & Son, a Kirkcaldy law firm, has the following list of partners: Brian Wood, David Wood, Angus Wood, and Charles Cant.

FOR those having trouble giving up smoking, we can heartily recommend two GPs in partnership in Birmingham: Doctor Gaspar and Doctor Pant.

GLENMAVIS Flying Club was able to announce that the pigeon-fancier who had gained second prize in their latest competition was a Mr H. Doo.

THE president of the Scottish Fishermen's Federation is Cecil T. Finn, MBE.

CREATORS of a CD-ROM on Interactive Homosexual Relationships – Michael Fitzpatrick and Patrick Fitzmichael.

A CHAP who has made a bit of a name for himself as a visual historian and artist on the subject of golf in St Andrews is a Mr Putter.

A DAVID Squibb directed the Trinity Boys Choir for the BBC's Guy Fawkes night special.

A LEADING authority on garden ponds is one Dr David Pool.

AN anaesthetist at Ayr Hospital is one Dr Sleap.

INVERARAY'S leading purveyor of venison is one J.F. Slaughter.

IN charge of the Health-in-Mind project in Saltcoats is a Mr George Nutman.

A FRENCH secret service agent mentioned in newspaper reports was a M. Alain Mafart. No doubt one of the silent but deadly school of spies.

DIRECTOR of a Channel 4 series, *Over the Rainbow*, on what it's like to be homosexual in America, was an Arthur Dong.

A PILOT at Manston Airport in Kent – a Mr Len Stall.

AER Lingus call all their planes after saints. Even the disembodied cockpits to be found in their simulator training facility at Dublin airport – all of which bear the name St Thetic.

IN a Glasgow schools football tournament one of the participating teams, Stonedyke primary, appeared on the scoreboard as St Onedyke.

A NEW crematorium in Cork is located in the Ovens district of the city.

SHORTLY after losing £23 million on short-term deposit with the BCCI bank, the Western Isles Council appointed a depute director of finance called David O'Loan.

INDEPENDENCE lager, the brand launched by Ian Lawson of the SNP and which carries heavy nationalist overtones, was christened Nats' piss by political opponents.

ENDELL Laird departed as editor of the *Daily Record* minus an accolade which some people in the newspaper trade thought would come his way. One of the last campaigns of his editorship was to raise a few million to build a children's hospice. This good work, it was thought, might well result in a knighthood. But when the honours list was issued, staff at Anderston Quay scanned the list but there was no elevation for Mr Laird. Hence the comment that was heard: 'The cry is no Sir Endell . . .'

SHOPS in the West End of Glasgow: greengrocer Roots and Fruits, fishmonger Tails and Scales, newsagent and tobacconist Reads and Weeds.

SPOKESMAN for the Soil Association is one Martin Trowell.

AT the Ministry of Defence we find a head of regional policy unit, M. A. Muskett.

ONE of the people at the Office of Fair Trading whose job is to deal with the Estate Agents Act is one Wendy House.

WYLIE & Lochhead funeral directors took over premises in Clarkston previously occupied by a dress shop specialising in apparel for diminutive South Side ladies. It was called Five Feet Two and Under.

THE Free Church sent a team of fund-raisers to the USA last century. The three people chosen to rattle the collecting box were Dr Begg, Dr Robb, and Dr Steel.

A TALK on Advances in Female Sexual Health was delivered by Dr A. Bigrigg and the whole event was sponsored by Upjohn, the pharmaceutical people.

A BRAND of toilet roll in Thailand rejoices in the name Sit & Smile.

NICKNAMES

THE village of Ballater has a strong tradition of nicknames. Brodie Hepburn, patron of the local Hayloft Restaurant, swears it is true that there is a local window-cleaner whose mother is of Arabian extraction and he is known as Sheik Ma Shammy.

DONALD, a chap from the South Lochs area of Lewis was wont to visit the bright lights and become involved in a ruckus on a Friday night after a dram or seven. Donald became known as Tensing due to the number of times he found himself inside a Stornoway polis Sherpa van.

CALUM MacLennan, a young Lewis lad spent so much of his hard-earned wages from the fish farm on mail-order designer gear that he became known as Calum Klein.

A CHAP called John in the Highland fishing hamlet of Mallaig had travelled the world, including a long spell in South Africa where he had enjoyed all the benefits that were part of the white man's lot during the apartheid years. He eventually returned to Scotland, bought a fishing boat, and took up prawn fishing among the genteel mariners of Mallaig. During many

a debate in the Fishermen's Mission or Chlachain Bar, John would sing loud and long the virtues of apartheid. He was duly awarded the ironic and not very politically correct nickname of John the Darkie.

A HOCKEY player named Rona, who was very committed and perhaps a bit on the tough side, became known as Testosterona.

FROM Tobermory we heard of a man called R. Slater who became known as Heid First.

A BARRHEAD lad called James Hughes had a slight speech defect and when asked his name would reply 'Jim Shoes'. He became known as Sanny.

TOM Bradshaw of Bellshill offers the story of a Ravenscraig steel worker who suffered from chronic eczema. His other defining characteristic was that he was a keen weekend fishermen and had a wee boat berthed in Girvan. He became known as Skinbad the Sailor.

A REGULAR customer at the Rodel Hotel on Harris has the nickname Nelson because he has a glass eye. When answering the call of nature, Nelson has been known to remove his glass eye and place it on the counter behind his glass of beer with the instructions: 'Look after my pint till I get back.'

On one occasion, a crew of visiting yacht people entered the bar while Nelson's Eye was on guard duty. A young lady in the company glanced at the pint glass, was confronted by a much magnified eye staring at her, and duly fainted.

A FORMER Navy man from Kilmarnock was called Sailor. (No slouches at the nicknames, the Kilmarnock boys.) Sailor had a glass eye which fell out when he dived into the deep-end at the town baths. He then became known as Sailor the Popeye Man.

ANOTHER monocular chap, who worked in a lower Clyde shipyard, was called Aladdin by his workmates because he only had one lamp.

A DUNBARTONSHIRE teacher by the name of Dunnion was known to his charges as Pickled. WE HEAR of a teacher called Ivan D'Inverno who was only 4ft 11in tall and was known as The Towering D'Inverno.

ANDY Goram, the Rangers goalkeeper was given the nickname Silkie after one of his many appearances on the front pages of the tabloid newspapers. An understanding of this name may be gained from a question on the TV comedy quiz programme

A Game of Two Halves. The panelists were shown four photographs – a Hibs jersey, a Rangers jersey, a Hearts jersey, and a pair of women's knickers – and asked to pick the odd one out. The answer was that Andy had never worn a Hearts jersey.

FOLLOWING a fashion set by rock star Prince, it was suggested there might be a comeback by Sydney Devine, the Scottish singer formerly known as Mince.

HIGHLANDER, a Scots nightclub entertainer, circulated venues with details of his act. As well as his Highland dancing, he is an accomplished drag artist, it says, appearing as a transvestite called Wilma Bumdoo.

A CHAP who had gone rather thin on top but had managed to hang on to three long strands of hair which he arranged across his bonce became known as Baldy Locks and the Three Hairs.

FROM a local authority office we heard of The Boomerang, a chap who was always promising 'I'll get back to you.'

IAN Donnelly of East Kilbride had a workmate called Cecil, short for Cecil B. De Mille, due to his habitual use of the phrase 'Let me put you in the picture.'

A REGULAR at a certain pub in Easter Ross, is known as Nimrod. because he is always looking for a sub.

BILL Nolan of Irvine pays tribute to his wife Mary whom he describes as 'wonder woman'. This is on account of how she is often left wondering where he is of an evening.

THE town of Campbeltown in Argyll is famous for the number and variety of local nicknames such as Biscuit Hips, Big Ebb and Wee Flo, Tear a Blouse, Knickers and Vest, Tartan Drawers, Neil the Bugger, and Shitey. Some of these appellations did not bear further investigation but one nickname, The Rat, wasn't as bad as it sounded. It had nothing to do with the man's personal qualities, simply that he had once escaped a sinking ship.

FOUND ON THE INTERNET

VIA the Internet comes the short-list for the Darwin awards, the point of which is to celebrate the fruits of four and a half billion years of evolution. Nominations are culled from the many little stories which prove just how clever us humans can be.

Among the nominees, many of them deceased at their own hands, are a man in San Jose who, 'using a shotgun like a club to break a former girlfriend's windshield, accidently shot himself to death when the gun discharged'.

KEN Charles Barger, 47, of Newton, North Carolina, wake-ned to the sound of a ringing telephone beside his bed. He reached for the phone but grabbed instead a Smith & Wesson .38 Special, which discharged when he put it to his ear.

A TORONTO lawyer, demonstrating the safety of the windows in his skyscraper office, crashed through a pane and fell 24 floors to his death. A police spokesman said Gerry Hoy, 39, fell into the courtyard of the Toronto Dominion Bank Tower as he was explaining the strength of the building's windows to visiting law students. Peter Lauwers, managing partner of the firm Holden Day Wilson, told the *Toronto Sun* newspaper that Hoy was 'one of the best and brightest' members of the company.

A NOMINEE who is still alive but may not be free to collect the award: Karen Lee Joachimi who was arrested in Lake City, Florida, for attempted robbery. She was armed with an electric chainsaw which was not plugged in.

BUT the winner was Larry Waters of Los Angeles whose boyhood dream of becoming a pilot were shattered because of his poor eyesight. Undeterred, he went to the local Army surplus store and bought 45 weather balloons and several tanks of helium. He attached the inflated balloons to a garden chair and, duly strapped in, cut himself loose from the rope which had been anchoring his device to the ground.

He expected to reach a cruising altitude of about 30ft. He actually levelled off at 11,000ft. Not being a daftie or anything, Larry had taken the precaution of taking with him a few sandwiches and a six-pack of Miller Lite. He also took an airgun to puncture the balloons and allow him to descend to safety. He decided not to use the gun in case his flying machine

became unstable and fell to earth.

By this time he had drifted into the primary approach corridor of Los Angeles airport. A United Airlines pilot radioed to report a man in a garden chair holding a gun at 11,000ft. As Larry drifted out to sea, a helicopter was sent in pursuit. A line was eventually attached to the chair and Larry was towed back to earth.

THE Internet is a useful place where age-old questions can be addressed, such as: why did the chicken cross the road? A current debate has produced such answers as:

THOMAS DE TORQUEMADA – give me 10 minutes with the chicken and I'll find out.

DARWIN – it was the logical next step after coming down from the trees.

EMILY DICKINSON – because it could not stop for death.

ERNEST HEMINGWAY – to die. In the rain.

SADDAM HUSSEIN – this was an unprovoked act of rebellion and we were quite justified in dropping 50 tons of nerve gas on it.

RONALD REAGAN – I forget.

ANDERSEN MANAGEMENT CONSULTING – Deregulation of the chicken's side of the road was threatening its dominant market position. The chicken was faced with significant challenges to create and develop the competencies required for the newly competitive market. Andersen Consulting, in a partnering relationship with the client, helped the chicken by rethinking its physical distribution strategy and implementation processes.

THE Internet offered a comparative guide to world religions.

TAOISM: shit happens.

HINDUISM: this shit happened before.

CATHOLICISM: shit happens because you are bad.

CHRISTIAN SCIENCE: shit is only in your mind.

HARE KRISHNA: shit happens, rama rama.

MOONIES: only happy shit happens.

EXISTENTIALISM: what is shit anyway?

CONFUCIANISM: Confucius says shit happens.

MORMON: this shit is going to happen again.

PROTESTANTISM: let this shit happen to someone else.

SEVENTH-DAY ADVENTIST: no shit on Saturdays.

CALVINISM: shit happens because you don't work hard enough.

BUDDHISM: if shit happens, it isn't really shit.

ISLAM: if shit happens, it is the will of Allah.

JUDAISM: why does this shit always happen to us?

STOICISM: this shit is good for me.

ZEN: what is the sound of shit happening?

RASTAFARIANISM: let's smoke this shit.

EUROPE'S search for a common language was reflected in this possibly apocryphal report:

The European Commission has just announced that English will be the official language of the EU rather than German which was the other possibility. As part of the negotiations, the British Government has agreed to some spelling changes which will be phased in over five years.

In the first year, the letter S will replace the soft C. Sertainly this will make the sivil servants jump with joy. The hard C will be dropped in favour of K. This should klear up konfusion and keyboards kan have one less letter.

There will be growing publik enthusiasm in the sekond year when the troublesome PH is replased with the F. This will make

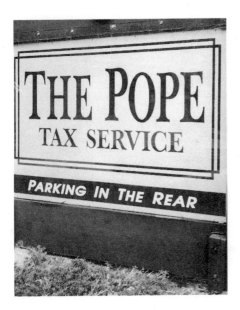

words like fotograf 20% shorter. In the third year, publik akseptance of the new spelling can be expekted to reach the stage where more komplikated changes are possible.

Governments will enkorage the removal of double letters, which have always ben a deterent to akurate speling. Also, al wil agre that the horible mes of the silent E in the language is digraseful.

By the fourth yar, pepl wil be reseptiv to steps such as replasing TH with Z and W with V. During ze fifz yer ze unesesary O kan b dropd from vords kontaning OU.

Similar changes vud of kors be aplid to ozer kombinations of leters. After zis fifz yer, ve vil hav a reli sensibl riten styl. Zer vil be no mor trubls or difikultis and evrivun vil find it ezi to understand ech ozer.

OTHER SPORTS

A GREAT moment not broadcast on BBC Scotland TV sport. The fragrant Hazel Irvine was doing a piece on rugby in Shetland. One of the Shetlanders was filmed running the line wearing a kilt and a Viking helmet. As part of her research, Hazel had been told that this zany character's nickname was Biscuit. 'Why are you called Biscuit?' she duly asked, at which point he lifted his kilt and said: 'Because it's a cracker.'

THE Wit and Wisdom of the Crowd: The scene was Twickenham during a break in play where Victor Ubogu was changing out of his ripped shorts. 'Victor Ubogu,' said a voice in the temporary silence. 'Not so much a name, more a bad hand at Scrabble.'

A LANGUAGE and That award to Craig Chalmers, captain of Melrose rugby club for a post-match summary of how his team won the McEwan's national league title by defeating Currie 74–10: 'In a game like this it is a matter of who makes the less unforced errors. We made less unforced errors and managed to force them into making more unforced errors.'

RUGBY World Cup Soundbite. The venerable Bill McLaren on BBC Radio 5 Live as a Tongan player was receiving treatment for an injured leg: 'He appears to be badly hurt, and what use is a hooker without a left leg?'

A SIGN in a Kilbirnie golf clubhouse: 'Members with outstanding balls should contact the bar staff.' It was nothing medical, we should point out, but simply that a number of golfers who had qualified for free golf balls by dint of scoring birdie twos had failed to collect their prizes.

WE are told the following events took place in Helensburgh Golf

Club but we can scarce believe it of that douce place. There were two Swedish golfers visiting and after a few beers at the 19th, a local was heard to say: 'Seein' as you're fae Sweden ah'll sing yis an Abba song . . .' And burst into 'Abbalong tae Glasgow'.

WE are sure this has never happened at any west of Scotland WASPish golf club but will pass on the tale as it was told to us. The club secretary is perturbed to see two chaps who are as black as two in the morning park their car and proceed to take their clubs out of the boot. He hurries down to ask them what they are doing in this private club. They explain that they had written to make a booking to play the course. The secretary says he will check. The records reveal that they had indeed booked so he returns to confirm that they had indeed written but through an error on his part, for which he humbly apologises, there is no chance they can play that day. He recommends

a perfectly adequate public golf course which is 'very close and you could leave here and be on the first tee in 10 minutes'.

The black chaps are not impressed and one asks: 'Would it make any difference if our names were Linford Christie and John Regis.'

'Of course,' replies the secretary. 'If you were Linford Christie and John Regis you could be on the first tee in five minutes.'

THE ETIQUETTE of golf clubs never fails to amaze and amuse. The extremely posh Glasgow Golf Club at Killermont extends its rigorous rules to the dirty bar, usually a haven for lawless and casually dressed members of golfing fraternities. Killermont goes so far as to reprimand members who try to use the dirty bar when they are too well-dressed. And they have struck a blow for decent standards of behaviour everywhere by decreeing that sandwiches may not be consumed while golfers are

Mrs Lang, who takes a size 4, had to settle for a size 6 stuffed with considerable quantities of toilet paper. They returned to Haggs Castle but, as she hobbled into the dining room, a further problem was identified. Her husband did not have a jacket and jackets are compulsory after 7.30 p.m. But spare jackets are kept in reserve for just such occasions and one was duly produced.

As Mrs Lang said: 'Neither my husband nor I have the slightest intention of pursuing a stage career, but his resemblance to Norman Wisdom (minus the bunnet) and my clown's feet were quite staggering. I hope we performed in a manner that was acceptable to the members of Haggs.'

having a pint in the dirty bar. Sweets are, however, permitted.

MORE on the mores of golf clubs and the lengths to which these self-important organisations will go to enforce their arcane rules. Moira Lang of Oban told us of a visit with her husband to Haggs Castle Golf Club in Glasgow. The Langs committed the crime of wearing casual clothing and comfortable sports shoes of the variety much favoured these days. The trainers were a problem. The Langs were not allowed to enter the dining room while wearing trainers.

They duly retreated to a relative's house nearby where 'proper' shoes were borrowed.

THE Callander golf club rule-makers have put themselves into a different class with their diktats on behaviour in the lounge and bar: 'Feet must not be placed on chairs or tables' and 'Chairs must not be tilted on to two legs while sitting on them.'

A LETTER from an angler to *The Field* magazine read: 'I have been fortunate to enjoy a week of stalking on Shiel deer forest for many years, but this season I was grounded because of a broken Achilles tendon. I decided to concentrate my efforts on the Shiel river in the hope of catching

a salmon. For the past 11 years they have eluded me, though not from lack of effort on my part, but I have now discovered the secret to success. On the Sunday we arrived, I tied an outrageously colourful fly which featured a tuft of my wife's pubic hair (theory being that pheromones might work as well on the old cock salmon as they do on me). Sure enough, on Monday morning and on the 11th cast, I hooked and landed a beautiful 4lb fresh fish. My problem now is not so much that I have run out of raw materials for my fly-tying, but what to call this superb new fly. Perhaps readers can help?'

The letter was headed 'A new Hairy Mary?'. We took advice on what this might mean from Paul Young, the kenspeckle TV angler. He said that a Hairy Mary is a classic angling fly made from dyed squirrel hair and various other materials. Paul does not know the lady after whom it is named. But he did suggest that the gentleman mentioned above might like to call his new fly, the Heriot-Watt.

Sometimes we wish we understood more about angling.

THE PAY POKE

'I WOULDN'T take a broken pay packet home to her,' is a phrase often used to describe a wife of frightening mien who has her husband totally under the thumb.

THE subject of the broken pay packet was raised by a reader writing of more prosperous days in Clydebank when there was a flourishing shipbuilding industry.

A local man bought himself a NCR accounting machine of the type used in wages offices. The reason for this arcane purchase became clear when the chap was found touring the shipyards on pay day with the machine in the back of his van. For 10 shillings (that's 50p in new money) he would print for his clients a replacement, less-remunerative pay-slip for those who wished to achieve some economic advantage over the wife. For a further sixpence (that's a tanner in new money) he would provide a fresh pay poke for handing over sealed and unopened.

THIS story provoked further examples of pay poke mythology.

SOME pay packets were designed with a semi-circular hole at the top which enabled the recipient to check the amount without breaking the seal. Hugh Ferguson of Cathcart tells us of an engineering works somewhere in Glasgow where an innovative employee perfected a technique using a split pin (a bit of kit not dissimilar to a lady's kirby grip). By inserting the pin and twirling it carefully, he could remove a bank note or two without breaking the seal. The pay poke was then returned, unopened, to the wages office with a complaint that the sum therein was deficient. No wonder Scottish engineers were at the leading edge of technology.

MARIE Murray of Campsie Glen tells us of an employee at the former Lion Foundry, Kirkintilloch, who was a bit of a Houdini

153

of the pay poke. His natural inclination was to take his wages to the pub and spend it on strong drink. His distraught wife would wait patiently at the factory gate. Unfortunately for her there were other exits. Eventually the wife and three daughters had every exit covered. Our man with the desire to ensure that his children should not have shoes, spent a week hacking through the undergrowth of a neighbouring garden and on Friday crawled his way, commando-style, to his own version of freedom.

A. MAIR of Dumbarton recalls the sophisticated way that employees of Babcock & Wilcox used to have of ensuring that the little lady did not get to keep all the wages to spend on rent, food, and shoes for the weans.

The company, in the paternalistic days of the 1960s, had a savings system whereby the workers could opt to put away a few pounds a week and this appeared in the deductions column under the heading 'Thrift'. There was a hard core of the men who opted for a high level of deduction and would then go and show the payslip to the wife with the words: 'Jist look what thae b******* took aff in thrift again.' The more hardened fiscal delinquents would turn up at the wages office on the Monday to withdraw the previous week's thrift money.

WEE Hughie is making his way home, clutching his pay poke. The drink is not Hughie's downfall but gambling and a bookmaker's heavy is on hand at the yard gates to relieve him of most of his wages. He is now faced with the more frightening situation of explaining the shortfall to his wife. He is on the Finnieston ferry and

EDDIE McDermid of Uddingston tells of the day the worm turned. The worm in question was a small timid man by the name of Jimmy who toiled in the local Caterpillar factory. He was married to a woman several sizes larger than he and was mercilessly bullied by her. Not only did his pay packet have to make the journey home unsullied but returning home at the end of every working day he was required to stand at the back door and remove his boiler suit. His better half would then pick it up with a pair of wooden tongs and deposit the offending workwear in the garden shed.

One Fair holiday, when the factory closed at lunchtime, Jimmy joined his workmates in the pub. He had a few drinks and, not being used to strong liquor, crossed the rubicon and opened the pay poke. At the end of his session, realising he was in a sheep-as-a-lamb situation, he converted the remains of his pay into half-crowns. On his return home he cast the coins into the kitchen with the words: 'Pick them up with your f****** tongs.'

Legend has it that Jimmy's wife saw him thenceforth in a new light and marital harmony ensued from that day.

spots the dear lady waiting for him on the other side.

Thinking as quickly as he can, he throws himself overboard, and swims about a bit before fetching up on the ferry slipway. He explains to Jessie that he almost drowned diving into the Clyde to retrieve the pay packet which had slipped from his grasp. But the brown envelope had floated away. Unconvinced, Jessie threw him back into the river, expressing the opinion that there were other things that floated as well as a brown paper envelope.

I REMEMBER POLLOK

I POPPED down to Pollok Free State, site of the Glasgow M77 tree wars, in the role of impartial observer. Then I discovered that they were building the motorway through my childhood. When I was a boy in the mid-1950s, the countryside started at my front door. Across the Brock Burn were some football pitches and then open ground stretching away up to a magical place we called the Gala Park.

Summer days were spent in the Gala Park. From morning till night. There was no need to go home for lunch. There was always a campfire with hot bubbling soup, courtesy of Galloway's the butchers who left their packets of Knorr on a window ledge which was vulnerable to young shop-

lifting fingers. Galbraith's the grocers were also very generous, albeit unwittingly. It was a busy life paddling in the burn, watching the soldiers from the nearby Army camp on manoeuvres with their girlfriends, and being chased by local farmers and greenkeepers at the Pollok and Cowglen golf clubs.

The beginning of the end came in 1957 when they tore up half of the football pitches to build Bellarmine school. We did our best at sabotage by putting sand in the fuel tanks of the bulldozers. But they built the school and took their revenge by incarcerating us in it.

The suburban blight spread rapidly. They built another school, called Craigbank, for the Protestants. It is now lying empty as, they say, Bellarmine will soon be, also. The Army camp was replaced by the National Savings Bank which at least gave jobs for those who survived Bellarmine and Craigbank. Commerce arrived in the shape of the Pollok Centre, a dreary monument to the consumer society which succeeds only in pointing up the poverty of the area.

I looked in to see the people who populate the campsite they call Pollok Free State and who believed they could stop the motorway. The Pollok Free State campsite was a wee boy's dream. In the very woods where the polis and the golf course greenkeepers used to chase us for playing cowboys and indians, there were now totem poles, tepees, tree houses – all sorts of esoteric artefacts erected by adults and fully sanctioned by police and planning department. They had a field kitchen which specialises in

157

When I visited, the conversation over cups of tea round the huge campfire was to a background of fiddle music. It's the sort of place where you can sit up all night round the fire. You get to flout authority. Your mum doesn't come looking for you to thrust you into the bath and then to bed. Even better than the Gala Park days.

And you get to meet interesting people. An American Indian chief, faith healers from Brighton, New Age protesters from all over the world. And Alsatian dogs. It wouldn't be Pollok without the Alsatian dogs. I walked from Pollok Free State over to what is left of the Gala Park. It is now a blasted heath, a bleak wasteland which can be improved only by putting a motorway through it.

What I am saying is that the battle to save my particular dear green place was lost long ago. They were fighting a losing battle, too, in Pollok Free State.

great pots of soup made from mounds of fresh veg. None of your shoplifted Knorr packets.

AND THE LORD DID SMITE THE TIMITES

FOR reasons which are shrouded in mystery supporters of Celtic FC are known as Tims. One school of thought is that the name comes from Tim Malloy, an archetypical Celtic fan. In a letter to *The Herald*, Gerry McSherry, a voluble commentator on matters Celtic referred to a phenomenon which he called 'anti-Timism'. It was thought appropriate that the Diary should investigate the anthropology of the Tim tribe.

For instance, when the Celtic board fall out are there intimperate exchanges? Is the tribe's favourite shampoo Timotei? Do classic scholars bemoaning behaviour of certain sections of the tribe exclaim: 'O timpora! O mores!'

NO PETS

NO BIKES

NO SOLICITORS

IAN Campbell of Stranraer reported that Rin Tim Tim, the Celtic Park dog, had died. Of distimper.

THE Revd Bill Shackleton asked if a shy psychiatrist of the Parkhead persuasion has a Tim id.

DAVID Petrie of Maryhill suggested that a favourite venue of the Timite tribe was bound to be the Tim Capsule in Monklands.

NEIL Brooks of Glasgow suggested that Catholic lorry drivers in America had formed the Timsters' Union.

JACK Shields of East Kilbride suggested that a blind follower of Celtic must be a Timbecile.

THE favourite drug of the tribe, according to Caroline Leitch of Glasgow, was Timazepam.

DAVID Donaldson of Glasgow told us that a Timite in France would no doubt be found chatting up the girls with the line: 'Je T'im Beaucoup.'

WHEN the Celtic board gets round to increasing the club's capitalisation it will be done, of course, on a Timshare basis, suggested Robert Beaton of Cowie.

THE ongoing controversy of the Celtic board would be remembered as Timgate, said Danny McCafferty of Duntocher.

FAVOURITE Tim films included The Tim Bandits and The Land That Tim Forgot. But the all-Tim favourite is the one about a disabled Tim – *My Left Foot* according to Dr Donald Lyons, of New Tim Mearns. Richard Roberts, of Kilmarnock, was more of a contimnental film buff, preferring Truffaut's Jules et Tim. Alan Kerr recommended the classic tales Tim Brown's Schooldays and Anne of Green-and-White Hooped Gables.

WEE STORIES R US

A CARD shop at the corner of Queen Street and Argyle Street in Glasgow has come up with a brilliant marketing concept – a section of cards with the heading, 'Say it with words'.

A GLASGOW working chap, after many years saving, treated his wife on their 25th wedding anniversary to a cruise on the QE2. After a few days at sea his wife, who was thoroughly enjoying the generous amounts of food and drink, met a more elderly, affluent woman on deck. They began talking and the Glasgow woman excitedly explained that this was her maiden voyage. The elderly woman said she was a regular traveller. She explained: 'My husband works for Cunard.' Slightly miffed, the

Glasgow woman replied, 'Aye hen, ma' man works f**kin' hard, as well.'

REALLY, this is not a joke about sex. It is a tale about Turriff folk.

A Martian couple are sent to study life on Earth. Their spaceship lands in a field near Turriff. Their arrival is noted by the farmer, who invites them up to the farmhouse for a cup of tea and a scone, as they do in Turriff. After the tea and scone, the farmer offers his visitors a dram, as they do in Turriff. A few drams later the farmer, who is an earthy sort of earthling, suggests that the Martian couple might like to indulge in a spot of wife-swopping, as they may or may not do in Turriff. Purely in the interest of their research, the Martian couple agree. Next morning the farmer emerges from the spare room and goes into the kitchen where his wife is busy cooking breakfast.

'Foo did ye get oan?' he asks her, as they do in Turriff. 'Jist fine,' she replies. 'Especially efter he explained that if I pulled on his left lug, his mannie would jist get langer and langer and langer. And if I pulled on the right lug, it jist got thicker and thicker and

162

existed in that category. 'Better narrow that down a bit. Put in an additional key word,' said the colleague. The word 'fiasco' was typed in, which narrowed the number of potential entries to 2192.

JUST when you think Scottish folk are getting too sophisticated with all this foreign travel, we hear a refreshing report from Glasgow airport. A plane which had brought a load of Scots home from Majorca could not depart with its next load of holiday-makers because two lifejackets had been nicked. They must have made a change from the more run-of-the-mill holiday souvenir.

A NAE Luck award to the Newton Mearns lady who was spotted attempting to add to her horticultural stock. The scene was a branch of the Abbey National which had been recently refurbished with an impressive array of greenery.

The Mearns matron surreptitiously produced a pair of scissors from her bag and, before you could say chrysanthemum, a cutting was in the bag. A cutting, it should be said, of an artificial plant that looks uncannily like the real thing.

thicker. Man, it was grand,' she said. 'An' foo did you get oan?'

'Aw richt, but I couldna get a wink's sleep for that Martian quine fiddling aboot wi' ma ears.'

A CHAP of the librarian persuasion was being given a demonstration of a CD computer system which can hold the entire year's stories from a newspaper. 'It's quite simple. Put in a key word,' his colleague advised.

He duly obliged, putting in the word 'Major'. The computer informed him that 2193 stories

A GATHERING of politicians and journalists were watching fascinatedly from a House of

Commons window as angry gay campaigners outside reacted to the vote not to reduce the age of consent to 16. As the demonstrators hurled bottles and tried to break down the Westminster doors, one onlooker asked: 'Do you think they're going to storm the building?'

'No,' replied another. 'But they might come in and redecorate.'

LORD James Douglas-Hamilton, former Scottish Office Minister for Quite a Lot of Things, will live in myth and legend. Lord James was on a visit to a Glasgow housing co-operative. And, at the request of the media, Lord James was carrying out a vox pop on the subject of the housing co-operative initiative. The replies were suitably enthusiastic. Apart from one Glasgow lady – a vision in headscarf, shopping bag, and sore feet. 'What do you think of the co-operative?' Lord James asked.

'Rubbish!' she retorted. 'Their shelves are aye empty an' you're far cheaper at Asda.'

LORD James is a gentleman of the old school. It was with some surprise that we heard, therefore, of a complaint by the lady driver assigned by the Scottish Office to look after him. A month after starting she complained to her supervisor: 'I can't work with Lord James any more.' The supervisor replied that Lord James could hardly be considered as a demanding employer.

'That's just the problem,' she replied. 'Every time we stop he gets out and comes round to open my door.'

A REPORT from an Easterhouse school whose office maintains a list of suspended pupils so that teachers can keep track of who

寶記飯店
PO KEE
RESTAURANT

shouldn't be in class. Most of the offences (theft, violence . . . the usual gamut of playground behaviour) on the list are straightforward enough. But one entry, FTFO, needs some explanation. It is used to describe miscreants who have been ordered to leave the school building for a previous offence but have sneaked back on to the premises. To the staff FTFO means Failure to F*** Off. Visiting officials are informed, however, that it means Failure to Follow Orders.

THE minutes of Inchinnan Community Council's annual meeting were commendably brief. We particularly liked the chairperson's report, which read in its entirety: 'Last year was a very quick and enjoyable experience.'

THIS story was stolen from Lord Willie Whitelaw, past captain of the Royal and Ancient. It concerns a golf widow whose husband has a habit of returning very late to the matrimonial home. She leaves a note on the kitchen table which reads: 'The day before yesterday you came home yesterday morning. Yesterday you came home this morning. But if today you come home tomorrow you will find I left you yesterday.'

CHARLIE, an acquaintance of the Diary, is a nice chap who does his bit to support the homeless. Every fortnight without fail he handed over 50p to the same *Big Issue* vendor whose pitch is adjacent to a pub which Charlie frequents. While handing over his 50p, Charlie declines to take a copy of the magazine. No disrespect to the *Big Issue*, he says, but it does not include racing form or information about fixed odds betting. One week he handed over the usual 50p and walked on, only to be hailed back with the words: 'Mister, it's gone up to 70p.'

WEMBLEY WAYS

THE match between England and Scotland in the Euro 96 championship was the first encounter with the Auld Enemy at Wembley for a decade. The occasion spurred Diary readers to recall Wembley tales of yore.

DAVID Montgomery of London was there in 1977 when the turf was stolen and the goalposts levelled. As the mayhem ensued he noticed the woman sitting next to him was near to tears. David tried to comfort her. 'Look, I know it all looks awful,' he said. 'But they don't mean any harm. They are just celebrating. Don't worry, it will be all right.' 'No it won't,' she sniffed, 'my husband's the groundsman.'

WE had an eye-witness account from an Alan Cochrane of Dundee of the scene that day on the pitch as Rod Stewart cavorted with other Scottish fans. One of the supporters took the oppor-

tunity to shake Rod firmly and emotionally by the hand. And at the same time relieve him of his Longines watch.

STEWART Smith of Hamilton had memories of the Wembley match in 1975 when England scraped home 5–1. 'We were still in

167

good humour as we trudged away after the match singing "We'll support you up to four . . ."'

Then Stewart and a cohort of Lanarkshire friends sought some diversion in a dingy club in Soho where one of the ladies who graced the stage could best be described as full-bodied. One punter, obviously touched, said: 'She reminds me so much of home.' Asked to elucidate, he explained: 'She's got an erse like the Whirlies roundabout.'

DURING the 1977 Scottish pillaging of Wembley Stadium. Fans bearing sections of turf were a common post-match phenomenon. Indeed, sitting opposite Mr Bate on the Tube back into the centre of London was a tartan-bedecked Bear with three sections of turf. But his pal had gone one better. He was clutching a battered and badly stuffed animal. 'This is the thing the dugs chase,' he explained. He had liberated the hare from the Wembley greyhound track. 'D'ye think the weans'll like it?' he asked.

IT is obviously something to do with the nightmarish score-line of 9–3. Gerry Gill, of Baronald Gate, Glasgow, recalls a fan leaving the stadium with a positive attitude. 'Mind you,' he said, 'when was the last time we took three goals aff England at Wembley?'

Smart alecs and those of a Leslie Welch disposition will know that the answer to this rhetorical question is 1951 when Scotland beat England 3–2.

DAVIE Ramsay offered the information that Frank Haffey of Celtic was only picked for the 9–3 because Lawrie Leslie of Airdrie had suffered a head injury. It is a shame Leslie was not patched up and put in goals, says Mr Ramsay, because 'a stitch in time would have saved nine'.

ALEX Reidford of Strathaven had a cautionary tale of wily Cockney ways which innocent Scots lads would do well to keep in mind. It was a Wembley fixture in the early 1970s when the public transport workers were on strike and the fans faced a bit of a hike to the venue. A group of supporters who had indulged in an extensive pre-match warm-up in a hostelry were making their way to the game, somewhat late, when they spied a large empty furniture lorry with its tailgate down. 'Hey, pal,' quoth one of the Scots to the man standing beside the van, 'Gie us a lift tae Wembley and we'll gie ye a quid each.'

The man considered the proposal briefly and agreed but pointed out that he would have to close the back doors completely to avoid the attentions of the police. Within minutes the fares were paid, carry-outs duly loaded, and the fans boarded the van. The Londoner put the tailgate up, helped by willing hands from inside. He then bolted the doors and, as Mr Reidford delicately put it, buggered off. It wasn't his furniture van.

TWO fragments of memory, although the first is not really in the category of memory. It involved David Wood of Uddingston watching (or listening to, it's hard to remember) the 1961 game in the company of his English brother-in-law. The deal was that they would have a dram each time either side scored. The final result was 9–3 and by the final whistle Mr Wood didn't really care about the score.

JAMES Laughlan of Larkhall was in a Tube train on the way back from Wembley and in the same carriage was a Scottish fan who was somewhat befuddled and was being looked after by a newly acquired English friend. On being woken up by a ticket-collector and asked where he was going, the confused Scot replied: 'Ah'm no sure. It's somethin tae dae wi plooks.' The London friend stepped in and said: 'He's trying to get to Hackney.'

KEN Gray of Ayr recalled a trip on the Tube to Wembley in 1973 when the fans were still allowed to have their own substantial portable cocktail cabinets.·

'What'll ye huv tae drink, hen?' a Scots fan asked a horrified posh English lady. 'No thanks, I only drink Campari,' she replied. 'Haw, Shuggy," the fan cried down the compartment, 'Pass up the Campari.' It was duly passed and offered, by the neck, to the lady with the words: 'Huv a slug o' that, sweetheart.'

ROBERT Beaton of Cowie sent in the story of a piper, an Inverness man, who went down for a Wembley match. Dressed in the full Highland kit, he booked into his digs and immediately began to get some bagpipe practice in. He tuned up and started marching up and down his room giving it laldy. After an hour, the landlady knocked on his door and said the chap in the room below was complaining about the noise. The Inverness man apologised and said he would take care of the problem. He took off his boots and carried on the practice marching in his stocking soles.

ROBERT Thomson of Unst in Shetland tells of a busload of kilted Scottish fans on their way to Wembley who stopped at Leicester for refuelling. One of their number, whom we will call wee Jimmy for the sake of anonymity, entered a baker's shop to buy some food to soak up the drink. The lady shop assistant entered into some badinage about whether he was a real Scotsman. She refused to believe he had nothing on beneath the kilt. 'Ah'll bet you that tray of cakes,' he said. She agreed. Up went Jimmy's kilt and out the door went one tray of cakes and other sweetmeats.

MOVING on from the Wembley years, we find ourselves with Scotland supporters in Rome in October 1993 where Iain Riddoch of Westhill, Aberdeenshire, is whiling away the hours before Italy beat Scotland 3–1 in a World Cup non-qualifying match. A squad of fans decide that a visit to Bonnie Prince Charlie's grave in the Vatican is in order. The party is

duly assembled, complete with wreath, and they march with some dignity behind a piper across St Peter's Square. The tourist cameras and camcorder were doing overtime at the sight of the proud Scots paying tribute to their uncrowned king. The ambience of this touching moment was only slightly spoiled by the fact that the piper chose to play 'The Sash'.

PARIS is the location for a tale by Alan Stewart of King's Park, Glasgow. It concerns two Scottish lads who were pursuing careers as buskers in the city of light. Their favoured location was

the entrance to the Metro station Charles de Gaulle. Having toiled sufficiently at the busking to earn the francs for a few beers and having consumed the few beers, the buskers remembered that Scotland were playing at Wembley that very day.

They embarked upon a scam which involved putting on tartan scarves and, in one case, removing a false tooth to give that authentic Scottish football fan look. Upon hearing a passing English accent, one of the buskers would start pressing the buttons on the illuminated map of the Metro and turn to the passing Englander tourist with the plea: 'Hey, pal, how d'ye work this thing?' 'Easy, just press the button for the station you want,' the English person would say. 'Aye, but ah cannae find Wembley and the game'll be startin soon.'

The conversation would continue with a rather stunned English person trying to explain to a Scots fan reeking a wee bit of alcohol that he was in Paris and not London. Our busker would ask what the bloody hell he was doing in Paris and say that the last thing he remembers was being a touch the worse for drink in Victoria bus station. Having received directions to the Gare du Nord and turned down the kind offer of a few francs, the busker would pop over to another part of the Metro where his pal was pulling the same stunt. Mr

Stewart assures us the story is true. He was one of those buskers.

NEIL Valentine from the South Ayrshire hamlet of Lugar recalled a visit to Wembley by a group of local miners. One of the party, on his first trip to London, got separated from the rest of the party and was wandering, lost and bewildered, in the environs of Piccadilly Circus. A passing policeman noticed his plight and asked in a broad Scottish accent if he could be of assistance. 'Thank Goad," said the Ayrshireman. 'Hae ye seen oany o the Ochiltree boays?'

GEORGE Liddle of Bishopbriggs told of the scenes in Euston Station in the wee small hours of Sunday morning after a Wembley match. Scots fans are strewn all

173

over the concourse waiting for the early train home. At 3.30 a.m. a particularly inebriated chap arrives singing patriotic verses at the top of his voice. He spots that the British Transport police are in attendance and decides that enough is enough. Finding one of the last remaining bits of wall against which to rest his weary bones, he announces to the railway polis: 'Ye can turn the lights aff noo. Ah'm the last wan in.'

SANDY Leitch was a Stenhousemuir supporter from Bonnybridge in the 1930s. Sandy looked forward to the biennial visit to Wembley and was blessed with a loving wife who actually put a shilling away from the house-keeping each week to fund the trip. In addition she gave him sixpence pocket money each time he left on the journey. One year, on his return, Sandy's wife asked how he had spent his sixpence. He explained that it was tuppence each way on the Tube to Wembley and that he had spent another penny on a chocolate bar. He confessed he could not account exactly for how he had spent the other penny. Raising her voice, she asked: 'You haven't been unfaithful to me, have you Sandy?'

A GLASGOW policeman told of the time he was on duty on the Sunday after the famous 1977 turf and goalposts Wembley. Some Scots fans of the criminal persuasion had taken the opportunity

during their visit to London to carry out a robbery at a jewellery shop. The tartan-clad raiders had last been seen making their getaway in a blue Transit van and the Metropolitan police duly alerted their Glasgow colleagues to look out for such a vehicle.

Our Glasgow polis, on duty in the London Road, duly spotted such a van loaded with football fans. When they were stopped and asked to open the back of the van the fans indeed appeared nervous. The doors were opened to reveal not a haul of jewellery but a van nicely carpeted in Wembley turf.

MIKE Shand of Elgin told of the fun his favourite tammy had while on Tartan Army manoeuvres in Hamburg for a World Cup non-qualifying match in 1969. The lucky tammy had seen service at such matches as Scotland's 3–2 defeat of England in 1967. Scotland lost to Germany on the occasion in question but this did not affect the abilities of the Jocks to celebrate. Mr Shand found himself trying to gain entrance to a dubious club in the Reeperbahn, at the instigation of a German press photographer, it should be said, who wanted a snap of a Scots fan in kilt and tammy embracing an exotic dancer. The club bouncer was not convinced about the concept but brought one of the dancers out to discuss the matter.

The upshot was that the lady was so impressed by the tammy that she borrowed it to use in her

act. Mr Shand, unfortunately, was not allowed into the club. The lady reappeared with the tammy stuffed down her impressive cleavage and the word was that the piece of tartan headgear had seen action in other places as well. That's why it was a lucky tammy, we suppose.

WHEN Scotland played England at Wembley during Euro 96 researchers from Caledonian University, Glasgow, were in London pubs carrying out a sociological questionnaire among the Scottish fans. One of the questions asked fans to name the two things they most disliked about Scottish football. One Rangers fan replied: '1. Sectarianism. 2. Fenian bastards.'